# ESTATE PLANNING GUIDE
# FOR NORTH CAROLINA

A Guide to Help Laymen Understand
Wills, Trusts, Power of Attorneys, Probate,
Living Wills, Medicaid and Taxes

J. Eric Kindberg

Lakeview Legal Press, Inc.
Charlotte, North Carolina

J. Eric Kindberg has been practicing Estate Planning and Administration in South Carolina since 1975 and in North Carolina since 1992. He earned his law degree from the University Of South Carolina School Of Law, his Masters Degree in Business Administration from the University of Alabama, and his B.A. from Vanderbilt University. His personal and family experiences have lead him to work exclusively in the areas of Estate Planning and Estate Administration.

Published by: Lakeview Legal Press, Inc.
5950 Fairview Road, Suite 808
Charlotte, NC 28210

ISBN – 978-0-9906144-0-1
First Printing 2014
Printed in the United States of America

# DEDICATION

To my wife, Lee, without whose support and encouragement this book would never have been written.

# Contents

# ACKNOWLEDGMENTS

I have not attempted to cite in the text all of the authorities and sources consulted in the preparation of this book. To do so would require more space than is available. The list would include departments of the county, state and federal governments, libraries, Web sources, and numerous individual clients.

Special thanks also to all of my clients who have allowed me to help them with their estate planning over the years. Seeing how good planning can salvage and strengthen family relationships has been an ongoing joy for me.

# ABOUT THE AUTHOR

Eric Kindberg is a Southern lawyer who has been licensed to practice in South Carolina since 1975 and North Carolina since 1992. He has been and remains passionate about encouraging everyone to get their estate legal affairs in order.

Eric was raised in Birmingham, Alabama and its southern suburbs. He attended Shades Valley High School and received a National Merit Scholarship to attend Vanderbilt University, where he earned a Bachelor of Arts degree in Psychology. He graduated in May, 1968, started the MBA program at the University of Alabama in June, 1968, married his (still) wife, Lee, in August, 1968, and was drafted by the U.S. Army in September, 1968. After nearly three years in the Army, including one tour of duty in Viet Nam as a Green Beret, Eric returned to the University in September, 1970. From there it was on to law school at the University of South Carolina from 1971 to 1975, and admission to the SC Bar in November, 1975. A family move to North Carolina led to another bar exam and admission to the NC bar in 1992.

Eric and Lee have a son and daughter-in-law who live in Charlotte, NC, and a daughter and son-in-law who live in Austin, TX with the two "perfect" grandchildren.
Eric can be contacted by email at
Eric@KindbergEstateLaw.com.

# DISCLAIMER

This book is designed to provide information about the subject matter covered. If you require legal, accounting or other professional assistance, the services of a licensed, competent professional should be sought.

Every effort has been made to make this book as complete and as accurate as possible. However, there may be mistakes both typographical and in content. Therefore, this text should be used only as a general guide and not as the ultimate source of estate planning law in North Carolina. Further, this book contains information on estate planning only up to the printing date.

The purpose of this book is to educate and entertain. The author shall have neither liability nor responsibility to any person or entity with respect to any loss or damage caused or alleged to be caused directly or indirectly by the information contained in this book.

**If you do not wish to be bound by the above, you may return this book to the publisher for a full refund.**

# FREE SPEECHES
## HELP SPREAD THE WORD

I never thought that I'd see two sisters team up to cheat their only brother out of his $3,000 inheritance. And then see the sisters fall out over the money less than a year later. But I did.

The possibility of inheriting money seems to bring out the mean, greedy streak in some people. I help prevent this destruction of family relationships by talking to folks about what Wills and Trusts and Power of Attorneys can do for them and their families. And I need your help to continue doing that.

If you know of a group that needs a speaker, please give them my information and give me their contact information. It can be a church group, civic group, social group, school group, book group, or any other kind of group. Almost everybody benefits from knowing more about estate planning, and having a chance to ask questions in a non-threatening forum.

I'm licensed to practice law in both North Carolina and South Carolina and will speak to groups in either State. Here's my information:

**J. Eric Kindberg**
**Attorney at Law**
**704-507-6444**
**Eric@KindbergEstateLaw.com**

I thank you for your help, as do the people I encourage to get their estate planning done. Whether by me or another qualified attorney. Just Do It.

# CHAPTER 1

# ESTATE PLANNING IN NORTH CAROLINA
### Exactly What Does That Mean?

You have all heard of the phrase, "Getting your affairs in order." Well, that is a simple but effective definition of estate planning. "Your affairs" do not begin when you die. Your affairs refer to your assets and relationships now, while you are alive, as well as your assets and the relationships you leave behind and influence when you die.

You do not know when you are going to die. You do not know if you will be incapacitated during your lifetime. As a result of that uncertainty, you need to plan.

The purpose of this book is to educate you, the lay person, about estate planning. This book is specifically designed to benefit you if you live in the state North Carolina. When it comes to estate planning, you may think that most states have similar laws, but that is just not the case. What you do not know can cause major problems, not just for you, but for your family for years to come.

## Estate Planning Involves Protecting What You Own

You have probably worked hard to accumulate what you have. If you do not plan properly, your assets can be taken away. For example, if you go to a nursing home, you could spend thousands of dollars each month on your care. Or, if you do not handle your retirement account properly, you could pay unnecessary income tax. If you do not plan for your future incapacity, your estate could be squandered away in a court-supervised guardianship proceeding. With all of the lawsuits in America today, it is even possible that you could be successfully sued, resulting in someone taking your entire estate away from you.

So, you can protect what you own while you are alive by:
- Protecting your assets from nursing home expenses;
- Minimizing your income tax;
- Avoiding a court-supervised guardianship proceeding in the event of your incapacity, and
- Protecting your assets if you are sued.

## Estate Planning Includes Taking Action to Protect Your Surviving Spouse

You may be thinking that you want to make sure that your husband or wife has financial security when you die. The

North Carolina laws that apply when a married person dies benefit the children more than the surviving spouse. It is important you take action to give your surviving spouse the security he or she needs.

**Example.** Bob inherited stock in ABC Inc., from his parents and the family home. Bob and his wife, Mary, are using the dividends from the stock to pay their monthly expenses. While Bob knows that he would want Mary to continue receiving dividends from the stock and living in the family home if Bob dies first, he never takes any action (such as getting his Last Will and Testament written) to protect Mary. Bob dies unexpectedly and because he had taken no action to protect Mary, it is possible that as much as two-thirds of all of Bob's assets, including both the house and the stock Bob had inherited, would go to Bob's children, and Mary is left trying to live on a fraction of the income they shared.

Because the children now actually own an interest in the family home, they can insist that Mary buy out their shares, or force a sale of the home so they can get their share in cash.

**Example:** Dad died without a Will and with the family home titled just in his name. One of his children, 19, was in the Army, serving in Germany. The son married a local girl, and told his mother that he wanted his share of the house. The law firm I was with at the time handled the Real Estate closing where the widow borrowed money to buy out her son's share. This was not a happy event.

You may be thinking that you and your spouse worked hard to pay for the home and you shouldn't have to get the permission of your children (or your spouse's children) in order to sell your home. You can plan ahead to avoid these problems.

Proper planning can even prevent your children from forcing your spouse to sell his or her house after you die. Again, the laws that apply in North Carolina when you die without planning typically favor the children over the surviving spouse.

Estate planning can protect your spouse by:

- Arranging for your assets to be available for your spouse after you die (as opposed to going straight to your children or to others);
- Arranging your affairs so your spouse will have the freedom to sell your home, other Real Estate, or other assets after you die (without having to get the permission of your children), and
- Eliminating the possibility that your children could force your spouse to sell assets or pay them their inheritance.

## Estate Planning Involves Taking Action To Protect Your Children

You have worked hard over your lifetime raising your children and providing financial security for yourself and, if you are married, for your spouse. You may be thinking that you would like to be able to provide one final gift to your children by leaving them an inheritance. How nice would that be to allow your children to have peace of mind in their remaining years because you were able to leave them an inheritance.

Or maybe you ride around in your car with one of those bumper stickers that reads, "I'm spending my children's inheritance." While that may be true, I'll bet that you'd rather have your children (or some other loved ones) inherit from you as opposed to your assets going to the government, the lawyers, or the courts.

Leaving assets to your children can be complex. Whether your children are young or old, rich or poor, married or single, you need to be aware of some important legal concepts that could jeopardize your children's inheritance.

If your children are young, you better have an estate plan. If you die before your children reach the age of 18 and you don't have a properly written Last Will and Testament, a judge will determine who will raise your children until they reach the age of 18. In addition, a judge will also determine who will control any financial assets that your children inherit, and, if any of those assets need to be spent on your children before they reach the age of 18 (for school expenses, living expenses, or for anything), a judge will have to approve those expenditures. This guardianship procedure is complicated and expensive.

If your children are married - or if they have been married, or even if they might get married in the future - you need to take action to protect their inheritance from their past or future divorces. You already know that many marriages these days end in divorce. What you may not know, is that if your children inherit from you and then get divorced, your child may have to share that inheritance with your daughter's ex-husband or your son's ex-wife.

You can also protect your children by arranging to minimize the tax that they pay at your death. A federal estate tax exists that could require your children to pay up to forty percent of their inheritance to the IRS. Capital gains tax and income tax can also be minimized or avoided through proper estate planning.

If you have children from a prior marriage, estate planning is a must. It is common for children to get nothing because their step-parent receives all the assets.

**Example.** James had three children from his marriage to his first wife. James and his first wife divorced. James later married his second wife. When James died, all of his assets went to his second wife. James' three children from his marriage to his first wife received nothing. Then when the second wife later died, she left all of her assets (including the assets she received from James) to her children.

Proper estate planning can avoid these problems because James could have arranged his estate plan to provide for his second wife, but also providing that at the second wife's subsequent death, assets would revert back to James' children.

Take action to protect your children:

- If your children are minors (or if they are 18 or over but unable to manage money to your standards), set up your estate plan so the court supervised guardianship proceeding is avoided and you dictate who raises your children and who handles their inheritance;

- If your children are older, take action to avoid leaving assets to your daughter-in-law or your son-in-law, particularly if your children have been divorced or may get divorced in the future;

- Arrange your affairs to avoid unnecessary taxes; and

- Protect the inheritance for your children, even if you are in a second marriage and you and your spouse each have children from a prior marriage.

As you read through the rest of this book, make notes about chapters that seem most important to you, so you can discuss those issues with your own experienced estate planning attorney.   One more example:

I once prepared the estate planning documents for a husband and wife.  Once prepared, I called their home on a Thursday, and asked the wife if they could come in the next day to sign everything.  She said, "We could, but my husband has a little cold.  He'll be better on Monday, and we can come in then to sign."  You can guess the rest of the story – yes, the husband unexpectedly died over the weekend, leaving a grieving widow and three small children, who now owned part of the marital home, among other assets.

None of us know how much time we have left.  Use yours wisely.

# CHAPTER 2

# POWER OF ATTORNEY
## Who Will Take Care Of Me And My Money?

### What is a Power of Attorney?

A Power of Attorney is a document that you sign that gives someone else (your Agent) the authority to act for you under certain circumstances.

**Example.** Ronald has two children, Adam and Eve. Ronald wants Adam to handle his financial affairs for him if he ever becomes incapacitated. Ronald signs a Durable Power of Attorney authorizing Adam to handle all of Ronald's financial affairs. Ronald also signs a Health Care Power of Attorney authorizing Eve to make health care decisions for him if he is unable to make them himself.

### Why Have A Power of Attorney?

Many people mistakenly believe that estate planning involves only getting their Last Will and Testament in place. Your Will does nothing for you in the event you become incapacitated during your lifetime. You need to make certain that you have the proper power of attorney documents in place.

There are many reasons that you should sign a properly drafted Power of Attorney as part of your estate plan:

- You will likely avoid the burdensome court-supervised guardianship proceeding that may be necessary when you become incapacitated and you haven't executed a proper Power of Attorney;

- You can designate the person who will handle your financial and health care affairs for you if you become incapacitated;

- If a guardianship is necessary, you can designate in your Power of Attorney who you'd want the court to designate as your legal guardian during your incapacity;
- You can authorize your Agent in your Power of Attorney to engage in tax planning and Medicaid planning techniques that he or she would not be able to perform in a guardianship proceeding.

## Different Types of Power of Attorney

All Powers of Attorney are not the same. You need to make important decisions before you sign your Power of Attorney.

## Limited Power of Attorney

A Limited Power of Attorney only lets your Agent act for you in accordance with the limits you set.

**Example.** You and your two sisters inherited your parents' house a year ago and it is now on the market. Someone has agreed to buy the home but you are going to be out of town on the date the closing is to take place, so you won't be available to sign the deed and other closing documents. Two weeks before the closing, you sign a Limited Power of Attorney authorizing one of your sisters to act for you in the sale of the property. Your sister cannot take any other actions for you other than acting for you at the closing. Your sister signs her name as your Agent, and you receive your share of the proceeds of the sale of the home.

## General Power of Attorney

1. A General Power of Attorney lets your Agent do anything you could do while alive and competent.
2. A General Durable Power of Attorney lets your Agent do anything you could do while alive, even if you are incompetent at the time.

By adding certain language to a Power of Attorney, whether Limited or General, either can become a Durable Power of Attorney. These days, every properly drafted Power of Attorney should contain this language. Most non-lawyers do not realize why this extra language is in their document. Many, and many lawyers, still refer to it as a General (or Limited) Power of Attorney, which is what we have done in this book. Do not worry, all of our Power of Attorneys contain language making them "durable."

**Example.**  While discussing your estate plan with your attorney, the attorney asks you who you'd want to manage your affairs, if at some point in the future you become incapacitated. Your attorney explains that most people execute a properly drafted power of attorney as part of their estate plan. He explains the benefits of avoiding the guardianship proceeding. You tell the attorney that you would want your spouse signing for you if you were unable to sign during your lifetime, and you state that you would want your oldest son to do it if your spouse were unable. Your attorney prepares a General Power of Attorney authorizing your spouse to act for you and providing that your son can act for you if your spouse has died or is otherwise unable to act for you.

If, for example, two years later you have a stroke and your house or vehicle need to be sold, it should be simple for your spouse (or your son, if your spouse is unable) to sign the necessary documents allowing them to sell your assets, if that is what is best for you.

### Health Care Power of Attorney

You can designate in your health care Power of Attorney who you would want making your medical decisions for you, if you are unable to make your own. You may have a Living Will whereby you declare your intentions regarding life-support machines, but your health care Power of Attorney covers other important medical decisions, too.

**Example.** Let's say you are in surgery or have some other medical condition and you do not have the ability to properly communicate your wishes regarding medical treatment to your physicians. If you previously signed a health care power of attorney, the physician can rely on the Agent that you named to make important treatment decisions for you.

### When Is Your Power of Attorney Effective?

The Power of Attorney that you sign can be effective immediately or it can "spring" into effect at a later date that you set.

### Immediate Power of Attorney

If your Power of Attorney is effective immediately (and most are set up this way), then the person that you designated to act for you can do so at any time. Your agent may present the power of attorney to a bank or other third party, or your agent may be required to record your power of attorney at the County Clerk of Court office if Real Estate is involved.

If the Power of Attorney is effective immediately, your agent can act for you at any time until the Power of Attorney is revoked or terminated.

## Springing Power of Attorney

Some people don't want to give anyone else the right to transact for them. However, you may want to set up what is commonly referred to as a "Springing" Power of Attorney, which springs into effect when you become incapacitated. Your incapacity will typically be triggered when doctors certify that you are unable to handle your affairs.

With a Springing Power of Attorney, you are the only person who can transact your affairs. However, when the doctors determine that you are unable, then the person that you designated as your Health Care Agent in your Springing Power of Attorney will be authorized to act for you. A Springing Power of Attorney typically avoids the difficult court-supervised guardianship proceeding.

## Terminating Your Power of Attorney

You may terminate your Power of Attorney at any time. If you never terminate your Power of Attorney, it will be terminated by your death.

**Example.** Your Aunt Nelda named you in her General Power of Attorney to handle her affairs. After Nelda had a stroke, you take care of paying her bills, selling her vehicle, and buying and selling certain pieces of Real Estate. If Nelda cannot make decisions about her medical treatment, the person named in her Health Care Power of Attorney would make them for her. When Nelda dies, both of the Power of Attorneys are terminated and neither you nor her Health Care Agent would have any more legal authority to handle Nelda's affairs. If Nelda appointed an executor in her Will, then the executor would have the authority to handle affairs after Nelda's death. If Nelda died without a Will, the court will likely appoint an administrator to handle Nelda's affairs after her death.

## Important Provisions For Your Power of Attorney

North Carolina law in the area of Power of Attorney is different from many of the other states. It is typically inadequate to sign a Power of Attorney which generally states that your Agent can do "anything that you could do."

In North Carolina, you must be express the things that you want your agents to do. If you want your agent to have the authority to do any of the following things, it must be expressly stated in the Power of Attorney. Express authority in the Power of Attorney document is required if you want your agent to have the authority to:
- Make a donation during your lifetime, either outright or to a trust;

- Accept or reject an inheritance;
- Take out a loan;
- Sell, buy, mortgage or lease something;
- Make health care decisions, such as surgery, medical expenses, nursing home residency, and medication.

Many improperly prepared Power of Attorneys do not include the express authority to make donations. When a person is incapacitated, it often becomes advantageous to a family for that person to make gifts to family members or trusts, either to avoid tax or perhaps to speed up the qualification process for Medicaid. If the Power of Attorney does not expressly authorize gifting, then the agent does not have the authority to make these gifts.

## Conclusion

Since there is good chance that you will not be able to handle your own affairs at some point during your lifetime, a properly executed Power of Attorney is one of the most important documents in your overall estate plan. Items to remember regarding your power of attorneys include:

- You designate who can handle your financial affairs upon your incapacity;

- You designate who can make medical decisions upon your incapacity;

- Having a Power of Attorney in place may avoid the burdensome court-controlled guardianship proceeding;

- Either of your Power of Attorneys can be general or can be limited to certain transactions or situations;
- Your Power of Attorney can be effective immediately when signed or it can be effective only upon your disability;

- In North Carolina, certain provisions must be expressly stated in the document, such as the authority to buy, sell, or donate.

# CHAPTER 3

# NORTH CAROLINA INTESTATE LAWS
## What Happens When You Die Without a Will?

You've probably heard stories about what happens to your assets if you live in North Carolina and you die without a Will. Maybe you heard that your entire estate goes to the government. Maybe you've heard that probate will take 20-30% of your estate. Perhaps you've heard that your children could force your surviving spouse to sell everything so that they can get their share. The purpose of this chapter is to describe what happens to your assets when you die without a Last Will and Testament.

### You and Your Spouse Have Separate Property

North Carolina is a NOT a community property state. In general, everything a married couple acquires during their marriage is owned by the spouse whose name is on the title, regardless of who earned it.

There are few exceptions to the rule that ownership is

determined by the name on the title. Most important is, if both husband and wife are shown as owners on a Deed to real estate, there is a presumption in North Carolina that this piece of real estate is being held as "Tenants by the Entirety." This means that when one spouse dies, the other automatically becomes the owner of all of that piece of property. However, if husband and wife do not want to hold property as Tenants by the Entirety, they need to tell their attorney when acquiring the property. It can be titled so each owns their share free of this automatic transfer policy.

**Example**. Bill and Mary are married. It is a second marriage for each of them. Mary owned her home before the marriage, titled in her name alone. Bill and Mary live in Mary's house for many years, paying off the mortgage with their funds. This house continues to be only Mary's asset, because it continues to be titled solely in her name.

This concept of "What's yours is yours and what's mine in mine" applies to all other property, including vehicles, bank accounts, stock brokerage accounts, company or business interests or stock. This is especially true with "family" businesses started by only one spouse where the other never receives any formal ownership interest. While most financial accounts require the owner to designate a beneficiary when the account is opened, if only one spouse is the owner, only that spouse controls what happens to those assets. Financial accounts in joint names, whether husband and wife or any two or more people, typically state that when one person dies, their share automatically goes to the survivor. If you do not want the other person on your account to automatically inherit the account, this needs to be arranged when the account is established.

If, in the previous example, Mary had conveyed the home to herself and Bill, as husband and wife, then North Carolina law would have considered that ownership by the Entireties. But, the "little home business" that she started on her own, which is now worth hundreds of thousands of dollars, would still be all hers, unless she transfers some ownership share to Bill.

Remember that:

- North Carolina is NOT a community property state which means that each spouse owns everything titled in their sole name.
- A spouse can have automatic inheritance of real estate if the title is held as husband and wife.
- You must understand the "standard" documents when taking title to an asset, to be sure the asset will end up where you want it to go.

All states, including North Carolina, have laws that determine what happens to your assets if you die without a Last Will and Testament. These laws are called "intestate" laws. If you have a valid Will when you die, you will have died "testate."

**If you Die in North Carolina Without a Will, Be Aware that North Carolina Has Different Rules Regarding Disposition of Real Property and Personal Property**

North Carolina intestate laws provide that when a married person dies, his property is divided among his wife, children, parents, and/or siblings, depending on what kind of property it is, and who survives whom. If a child has predeceased the parent, but left descendants (i.e. grand-children, great-grandchildren, etc.) surviving, the child's share will pass down his line to his living descendants. In this Chapter, whenever we say "the child survived" that also means "or his descendants survived."

For REAL PROPERTY, here is what the surviving spouse ends up with:

If there in only one child, that child inherits one-half of the real estate and the surviving spouse takes one-half.

If there are two or more children, the children equally divide two-thirds of the real estate and the surviving spouse takes only one-third.

If there are no surviving children, but there is a surviving parent, the parent(s) get one-half and the surviving spouse takes one-half.

If there are no surviving children or parents, all the real estate goes to the surviving spouse.

For PERSONAL PROPERTY, here is what the surviving spouse ends up with:

If one or more children survive, the spouse gets the first $60,000 and

1. If only one child survives, each takes one-half of the balance over $60,000
2. If more than one child survives, the spouse only gets one-third of the balance over $60,000.

If no children, but at least one parent survive, the spouse gets the first $100,000 and one-half of the balance over $100,000.

If there are no surviving children or parents, all the personal property goes to the surviving spouse

In North Carolina, a child legally becomes an adult at age eighteen. If a child is eighteen years old or older, his/her share is due to them immediately. Even worse, the share of a child under age eighteen must be held in trust, used only for the child's benefit, and yearly reports must be made to the

Court by the trustee to prove how the money has been spent and managed.

For example: Remember Mary and Bill's second marriage? Mary had a daughter, Myra, from her first marriage and Bill had a son, Ben, from his first marriage. Also, Mary and Bill had a son of their own, Trey. When Mary died suddenly, without a Will, Myra was 16, Ben was 20, and Trey was 12. Since Mary has two children, Myra and Trey, they inherit two-thirds of Mary's real estate and Bill gets the other third. Mary's house, still in her name alone, now belongs one-third to Bill, one-third to Myra and one-third to Trey. Bill will get the first $60,000 in personal property from the estate, but only one-third of the balance. Because Myra and Trey are both minors, their shares are to be held in trust, under court supervision. Myra's biological father, Percy, applies to the court to be appointed trustee of her assets. Since Percy also now has first right to raise Myra, he asks the court to give him custody of her, and to order the house sold and converted to cash to go into her trust. Bill has potentially lost his wife, step-daughter and home all at the same time. And is about to incur significant attorney's fees to work out all of these issues.

When you die intestate in North Carolina, your spouse might only inherit one-half or two-thirds of your assets, with your children or child getting the rest. When teenagers may have the right to demand tens or hundreds of thousands of dollars from the surviving spouse, it is traumatic to an intact traditional family. It is much more destructive to today's blended families, where these funds could be controlled by an ex-husband or ex-wife for years, or where the surviving spouse would be under court supervision and the harsh scrutiny of a child's biological parent before giving the cash and property to the child at age eighteen.

## You're Married, Have No Children and Die Without a Will.

If you're married, have no children and die without a Will, the surviving spouse is not guaranteed an easier time. In this case, one half of your estate goes to your spouse, and the other one-half goes to your parent or parents. So, how well do you get along with your in-laws?

**Example.** George and Debbie marry and live in Debbie's lake house, which she inherited from her father's estate. Debbie dies without a Will and without children. Now George owns one-half of the house where he lives (and any other real estate Debbie owned) and his mother-in-law owns the other one-half. George also gets the first $100,000 of personal property, but must give one-half of everything else Debbie owned to his mother-in-law.

### You're Single and You Die Without a Will

If you're not married when you die, or you have survived your spouse, and you die without a Will, your assets will go to your children in equal shares. If you don't have children, your assets will go to your parents, in equal shares, or to the survivor of them. If you parents don't survive you, then your assets will go to your brothers and sisters. If any of your brothers or sisters died before you, then that sibling's share will go to that sibling's children. If you find yourself in an estate like this, please consult a good Probate Lawyer.

See Chapter 10 – THE PROBATE PROCESS for full details on what it takes for the assets to get transferred to the heirs.

### Are Any Taxes Due When Someone Dies Intestate?

North Carolina eliminated its Inheritance Tax effective Jan. 1, 2013. Congress has imposed a federal estate tax on large estates. For deaths occurring in the year 2014, the first $5,340,000 in value is exempt from the federal estate tax. The estate tax rates are about 40% of the estate that exceeds the exemption amount. When a married person dies intestate, there is often no getting around this estate tax.

**Example.** Bill and Mary owned $8,000,000 in property. Bill had another $4,000,000 in separate property. Bill died intestate during 2013 when the estate tax exemption was $5,340,000. His estate equals $8,000,000 ($4,000,000 joint property plus $4,000,000 separate property). His estate owes about $1,100,000 in federal estate tax to the IRS - due within nine months of Bill's death.

The big problem was that Bill died intestate. If Bill had a proper Will written, there would have been no estate tax (due to a provision in our tax code which allows there to be no tax due upon the death of the first spouse to die - if the Will is written correctly).

## Conclusion

When a North Carolina Resident Dies Without a Last Will and Testament:

- North Carolina intestate laws favor the children over the spouse;
- If you're single when you die, your assets will go to your children, and if you don't have children, your assets will go to your parents, if surviving, or to your brothers and sisters;
- An administration will usually be necessary to transfer ownership of your assets; and
- Federal estate tax may be due if you have a large estate (over $5,340,000 for death occurring during 2014).

# CHAPTER 4

# YOUR LAST WILL AND TESTAMENT
**Maybe Your Family's Most Important Document.**

Your Last Will and Testament (also referred to as your "Will") is one of the most important documents you ever sign. You've spent your lifetime saving and investing for yourself, your family and your loved ones, and your last will and testament allows you to leave your possessions behind to the people that mean the most to you.  For many years, it was the primary method of passing wealth to the proper people.

**Reasons for Writing a Will**

There are a number of good reasons why you should write a Will, including but not limited to:

- Designating who you want your assets to go to when you die
- Designating the executor or co-executor of your estate
- Minimizing or avoiding federal estate tax
- Providing for contingencies that might occur such as a

spouse or a child predeceasing you

- Making it easier for your spouse to sell assets you leave him or her
- Establishing testamentary trusts for the benefit of those heirs who might need help managing their inheritance

## What Makes a Will Valid in North Carolina?

For a Will to be valid, it must be made in a form that is expressly authorized by North Carolina law. In North Carolina, there are two forms of Wills: Holographic and Statutory.

## Holographic Will

A holographic Will is a document entirely written, dated, and signed in your handwriting. Your holographic Will must be signed at the end of the Will. The holographic Will is subject to no other requirement as to form. It does not need to be witnessed or notarized to be valid.

While holographic Wills are valid, they are not recommended. Lay people typically do not have the expertise to properly draft a Will. While it's easy to create a holographic Will that is considered valid, it is difficult to draft a Will that covers everything that needs to be covered with clarity. The improper inclusion or exclusion of one word can cause ambiguity which often leads heirs to argue. Considering its importance, it's widely believed that you should hire an attorney and have your attorney prepare your Will using the proper legal language to document your intentions.

### Statutory Will

As opposed to the Holographic Will which is entirely in your own handwriting, the statutory Will is typed. We refer to it as a "statutory Will" because it is signed by you and two witnesses, as the North Carolina statutes require for a valid Will. This is the only type of Will we will talk about for the rest of this Chapter, and refer to it simply as "your Will." You sign your Will at the end, while two witnesses watch you sign, and the three of you watch each other sign. If you stop with this step, you will have a valid Will, but, to probate your Will, one or more of the witnesses will have to testify in Court that they saw you and the other witness sign this Will. Actually finding these witnesses many years from now, when your Will is being submitted to the Probate Court, is very difficult. So, by having your Will properly notarized, it becomes a "self-proving" Will, and no further testimony from witnesses is required to probate it in North Carolina. Your attorney can help ensure this signing process is done properly.

But, remember, that this North Carolina "self-proving" feature may not be effective if you move to another state. You need to check with an estate planning lawyer there to be sure.

## Important Provisions to Include in Your Will

The meat of the Last Will and Testament is typically in the bequests (also called "dispositions"). In North Carolina, bequests in Wills are classified as specific or general.

A general bequest is one in which you bequeath a fraction or a certain proportion of the estate, or a fraction or certain proportion of the balance of the estate that remains after specific bequests.

An example of a specific bequest of cash is as follows: "I leave to my nephew, Austin H. Johnson, the sum of twenty-five thousand dollars ($25,000.00), cash."

Another example of a specific bequest is of real estate, such as "I leave to my son, Jack Jones, Jr., all of my interest in the property located at 123 Florida Avenue, Charlotte, North Carolina." It generally is not necessary to list the complete legal description of the property when including a bequest of real estate in your Will.

Sometimes people make bequests of corporate stock in their Will. Example: "I leave 1,000 shares of ExxonMobil common stock to my grandson, Tim Jones." You may also want to make a provision in this bequest so that if the stock splits, or if the capital structure of ExxonMobil changes (such as if they are merged into another company), then this bequest would include those additional shares acquired through the stock split, merger, or acquisition.

Many of the Wills that we prepare do not include any bequests of particular assets. A husband's Will may provide, in general, that he leaves a life estate in everything he owns to his wife, with the remainder to his children. If you are not married, your Will may provide simply that all of your assets at the time of your death will be divided equally among your children, without listing the specifics of any of the assets that you currently own.

**Naming your executor**

Besides providing for the proper bequests, naming your executor may be the most important provision in your Will. It's your executor's job to gather all of the information on the assets that you own at the time of your death, hire an attorney, make decisions regarding the sale of your assets such as your home, vehicles, stock and other assets, if necessary to pay estate debts, and oversee the distribution of assets to the heirs.

The executor must comply with all of the North Carolina laws that pertain to him. Penalties and personal liability can result from an executor failing to perform within the required laws. A good executor can provide for an orderly disposition of assets, while a poor executor can cause your estate to drag on for months or years unnecessarily.

Who should you name as your executor? That's a good question. It should be someone you trust, and someone who is organized, fair and trustworthy. If you are married, you may want to name your spouse as your executor and one of your adult children as your alternate executor.

If you don't have a spouse or adult child that would make an appropriate executor, you can name a trusted friend or other relative to serve as your executor. You could also name a corporate trust department, CPA, attorney, or other trusted advisor as your executor. You can also name two or more people to serve as co-executors. If you have two children, you could name them as co-executors. Many parents do this because they don't want to hurt a child's feelings by leaving them out. Don't name co-executors unless you feel that they can work well together.

## Guardians for Minor Children

Parents with children under the age of eighteen need to write their Will so they can designate who will raise the children if the parents die before their children reach the age of majority (which is age18 in North Carolina).

In North Carolina, you can designate who you want your children's "guardian" to be if you and the other parent die before the child reaches the age of 18. If the parents are divorced, the last surviving parent has the right to designate who will be the minor child's guardian. The failure to designate the guardian for your children will result in a judge designating a guardian. Your choice for who can best raise your child or children may be different than a judge's choice.

## Using Trusts in your Will

Many people include trusts in their Wills. These trusts are commonly referred to as "testamentary trusts" because the trust is included in your last will and "testament."

While there are many uses for testamentary trusts, some of the most common include (1) providing for minor children; (2) protecting young children and grandchildren from themselves; (3) protecting your children from their divorces; (4) married couples using trusts in their Wills to avoid federal estate tax.

## Creating a Testamentary Trust for Young Children

If your children are young, or if they are not yet mature enough to handle a lump sum inheritance, then you should designate in your Will that when you die, your assets will be placed in trust. This helps ensure that your child's inheritance will be managed by the right person and used for the right reasons. A testamentary trust for minor children will also avoid the expensive and difficult guardianship proceeding which applies when a minor inherits property.

**Example.** Mark and Colleen have two minor children. Mark dies unexpectedly. Colleen decides to sell their home, which was just in Mark's name. However, since Mark did not have a Will which should have included a testamentary trust for their two children, Colleen was prevented from selling their home right away until she paid thousands of dollars in attorney fees and court costs to get court permission to sell the children's interest in their father's home and to get herself confirmed as the guardian of the children's inheritance.

If Mark, in the previous example, had written a Will which had included a testamentary trust for his children naming Colleen as trustee, then Colleen would have been able to sell the home shortly after Mark's death without having to spend a fortune on the difficult guardianship proceeding. Title to the home would have been changed into Colleen's name as trustee of Mark's children's trust, and Colleen would have been permitted to sell the home without having to get court approval to do so.

## Prevent Your Children and Grandchildren From Wasting Their Inheritance

An inheritance is typically not earned. Children and grandchildren often look at an inheritance as a freebie. You often read about lottery winners squandering away their winnings. People who receive an inheritance are no different. Since they did not work for or earn their inheritance, they don't value the money as much as you may value it.

**Example.** Leonard and Jackie worked their lifetime to build their estate of $600,000. They clipped coupons, bought items that were on sale, and avoided travel, eating out and other luxuries because they said these things were "too expensive." When Leonard and Jackie died, their two children each inherited $300,000. Their son, Billy, immediately purchased a new boat, a new truck, and many other items that years later had no value.

Leonard and Jackie could have arranged their Wills so that upon their deaths, their assets would have been transferred to a trust. Leonard and Jackie could have named a trustee (either an individual or a corporate trustee) to manage the assets for their children. The trust might say that the children receive all of the income from the trust assets, and the trustee can give the principal to the children for their health, education or general welfare. Perhaps the trust would also provide that the children would receive one-half of the trust assets when they reach the age of forty, and the rest of the trust assets when they reach the age of fifty.

## Protect Your Children from Their Divorces

The divorce rate is higher now than it was 30 or 40 years ago. While it's uncommon for a couple that has been married for 40+ years to get divorced, it is common that one or more of their children will be getting divorced.

By definition, an inheritance that your child receives is his or her separate property. However, your child's inheritance will quickly become joint property co-owned with your son-in-law or daughter-in-law unless it's handled properly. If your son or daughter later gets divorced after receiving this inheritance, he or she may be required to split this inheritance with his or her ex-spouse.

**Example.** Jason received an inheritance of $400,000 from his parents. His parents saved their entire lifetime so Jason could benefit from the inheritance. This inheritance initially is Jason's separate property. Jason invests the money. These investments produce interest and dividends. The interest and dividends from Jason's separate property are still Jason's separate property unless he co-mingles it with other jointly owned property (like a joint checking account). The joint property and separate property get mixed up together so that no one can accurately determine what is separate property and what is joint property. When this happens, it all becomes joint property which can be divided between Jason and his wife by a North Carolina Family Court.

One way to protect your children from having to split their inheritance when they divorce is to provide that the inheritance for each child of yours will be put in trust. This will make it more likely that the inherited assets will not be commingled with joint property that your child owns with his or her spouse.

### Using a testamentary trust to avoid estate tax

Married couples often include testamentary trusts in their Wills to help avoid estate tax. The estate tax exemption for the year 2014 is $5,340,000, so far fewer families are subject to this tax than before when the estate tax exemption was $600,000.

Nonetheless a married person can leave his or her estate in trust, name the surviving spouse as the income beneficiary of that trust, and follow other requirements, and there will be no federal estate tax required to be paid at the death of the first spouse to die. This trust is commonly referred to as a bypass trust or a QTIP trust (full name: a Qualified Terminable Interest Property Trust). This estate tax avoidance technique can also be accomplished by leaving your spouse a life estate in your assets with the remainder to your children or whoever you wish.

### Other common provisions in Wills

**Survivorship provision.** Many people ask, "What if I leave an inheritance to someone and that person dies right after me? Well, you can include a survivorship provision in your Will so that you can control where the inheritance goes if your legatee dies right after you. You can provide in your Will that the bequests in your Will are not effective unless the legatee survives you for a certain period.

**Advancements.** Sometimes a parent with more than one child will, during his or her lifetime, financially help one child more than the other. The parent may feel that it's fair to reduce the inheritance of that particular child that received gifts during the parent's lifetime. The parent may provide in his or her Will that certain gifts made to children will be considered an advancement so that those gifts made to those children will be counted as an advance on their inheritance.

## Provisions Not to Include in Wills

There are certain things related to planning for death that should not be listed in the last will and testament. Your Will may not be read until days or even weeks after your death when it's too late to abide by your wishes. The following are examples of items that should not be listed in your Will.

**Organ Donation.** If you wish to be an organ donor, you should do so by signing the necessary forms provided by the Donate Life North Carolina which is the State organ donor database, as well as documenting that you are an organ donor when you get a new North Carolina Driver's License

Decisions regarding life support machines. Your living will

is the proper place to document your decision regarding life support machines, not your last will and testament.

**Beneficiary Designation items.** Individual retirement accounts, 401(k) plans, life insurance and annuities are transferred to the persons designated on your beneficiary designation form held by the financial institution or insurance company. Do not make a bequest of an IRA in your Will.

**Example**. Don has an IRA worth $250,000. In his Will, he stated that he wanted his IRA to go to his son, Jason. However, when Don opened his IRA account, he named his daughter, Emily, as the beneficiary of his IRA. After Don dies, the financial institution will deliver the IRA funds to Emily, even though Don stated in his Will that he wanted those funds to go to Jason.

**Personal effects.** The proper disposition of personal effects can be tricky. It's simple to divide a $100,000 bank account between four children (each child gets $25,000), but it's not so simple to divide up your jewelry, china, furniture, tools, guns, family photos, and other personal effects among multiple heirs. There are two ways to provide for the disposition of your personal effects: inside your Will or outside your Will.

### Disposing of your personal effects in your Will

One way to dispose of your personal effects is to make bequests of these items in your Will. You might say something like, "I leave my diamond engagement ring to my daughter, Jenny." Or you might say, "I leave all of my tools to my son, Jason."

Disposing of your personal effects in your Will can be burdensome. You have to list all of these items in your Will and you have to list who you want to inherit these items. If you change your mind or if you acquire additional items that you'd like to bequeath, you have to change your Will.

However, if you think there is a chance that your heirs may fight over your personal belongings, then it may be best if you bequeath them in your Will, particularly if they have significant fair market value or significant sentimental value to your heirs.

## Disposing of your personal effects outside your Will

Some people will attempt to dispose of their personal effects outside of their Will. They might place a sticky note on each item which states who gets each item, or they may make a separate list in their own handwriting and change it from time to time. Or they may simply ask their children to work it out, or take turns picking items. There is no limit on the number of ways personal items can be passed along to your loved ones. This informal method can work well, particularly if your heirs get along well and can agree on an orderly disposition of these items.

Whichever way you choose to dispose of your personal items, it's important to communicate your desires now rather than leave it up to your heirs, or your executor, to make all the decisions.

## Conclusion

When you prepare your Will, it's important to keep these things in mind:

- There are two forms of valid Wills in North Carolina: holographic and statutory. Most Wills are statutory.
- Properly describing your bequests may be the most important part of your Will.
- Choosing your executor is also an important decision to document properly.
- It may be helpful to include a testamentary trust in your Will to
    - Easily manage property of young children
    - Protect young adults from themselves
    - Make your child's inheritance divorce proof
    - Minimize your Federal Estate Tax burden
- Other important provisions to include in your Will are guardianship provisions, survivorship provisions, contingent equests, and whether you want lifetime gifts considered as advancements.
- There are certain provisions that should not be in your Will, including, funeral arrangements; organ donation

wishes; life support machine use; and bequests of items containing their own beneficiary designations, like IRAs, bank accounts and brokerage accounts.

# CHAPTER 5

# TRUSTS

**Trusts can be a great tool—when used for the right reasons**

Trusts are sometimes complicated for the lay person to understand. But when used properly, they can be a valuable estate planning tool. Some of the common uses for trusts include: avoiding probate, minimizing federal estate tax, protecting your children from squandering their inheritance, provide for grandchildren's education or other needs, protect your spouse from your children of a previous marriage, protect your children of a previous marriage from your spouse, protecting the inheritance of a special needs child, and much more.

## What is a trust?

A trust is defined as a relationship which results when someone transfers title to an asset to a person whose job it is to administer it for another.

**Example.** In George's Will, he made a bequest of $50,000 to his son, George, Jr., as trustee of a trust for the benefit of George's grandson, George III. George provided, among other things, that the principal of the trust could be used for the health and education of George III, and George also provided that if the assets had not been used by the time George III reached the age of thirty, then the trust would terminate and the remaining trust assets would be distributed to George III. When George later died, a trust account was established and George, Jr., managed the account as trustee.

Who are the people involved in a trust?

Every trust has one or more settlors, trustees, and beneficiaries. The Settlor is typically the person who sets up the trust. In the previous example, George is the Settlor. The Trustee is the person who manages the trust assets. In our previous example, George, Jr., is the Trustee. The beneficiary is the person who benefits from the trust. George III is the beneficiary in our previous example.

What are the most common uses of trusts?

There are many uses for trusts in North Carolina. The following are some of the more popular uses of trusts.

## Revocable Living Trust

While the revocable living trust has been a popular estate

planning tool around the United States for decades, its popularity in North Carolina has intensified in recent years. Generally there are three reasons why the revocable living trust is a popular estate planning tool.

1. The properly funded living trust can avoid attorney costs and court costs involved in settling your estate through the court-supervised North Carolina Probate proceeding;
2. Distributing assets after death to beneficiaries of a living trust is faster than distributing assets to heirs in a North Carolina Probate proceeding; and
3. A North Carolina Probate requires a detailed public listing of all your assets and debts when you die. A living trust can be settled without the necessity of a public detailed listing of your assets and debts.

## How are Revocable Living Trusts Used?

**Example.** Charlene has three children. Charlene went through a difficult and lengthy probate when her father died and she wants to make sure that her children do not have to go through a similar process when she dies. Charlene sets up a revocable living trust, naming her three children as equal beneficiaries at her death. Charlene names herself as the initial trustee, and she names her daughter, Karen, as the successor trustee to be in charge when Charlene dies. Charlene reserves the right to change or revoke her trust at any time, hence the name "Revocable Trust". Charlene transfers her real estate and her investments to her trust. When Charlene dies, Karen immediately disburses the investments and the real estate equally to Charlene's three children. No probate was necessary because no assets were titled in Charlene's name which would require probate court orders to transfer.

One major use of a Revocable Living Trust is as a probate avoidance tool. If your assets are titled in your name when you die, your assets titled in your name will be frozen, and your family will have to go through probate and obtain court orders which order banks, financial institutions, and others to transfer your assets to your Executor. Then your Executor can distribute assets to your beneficiaries. If your assets are titled in the name of your trust, your successor trustee will have immediate access to your assets and will be able to sell or distribute them to your beneficiaries that you named in your trust – no probate is necessary to transfer these assets after your death.

## Avoiding North Carolina Probate

Many years ago it was determined that the courts must oversee the distribution of a deceased person's assets to their heirs. In North Carolina, this court-supervised procedure is known as "Probate."

Having the courts oversee the distribution of your estate to your heirs may not be the most efficient way for your family to settle your estate. Courts are well-known for having inherent delays and costs.

In most Living Trust arrangements, the parents are the Settlors, the initial Trustees, and the first beneficiaries. A successor trustee or co-trustees are designated (often an adult child or children), and the children are designated as the remainder beneficiaries – to receive the trust assets after the parents die. When the parents die, trust assets are not frozen and trust assets do not have to go through a court-supervised Probate procedure to be transferred. The trust instrument and trust law permit the successor trustee to distribute the trust assets in accordance with the instructions provided in the trust instrument.

## What Savings Result From Avoiding Probate?

That's a difficult question to answer. There is no standard for Probate costs in North Carolina. In part, it depends on the value of the personal property (i.e. everything except real estate) that passes through the estate versus how much passes outside of the estate. Probate costs always include court filing costs and attorney fees. There is no standard for attorney fees.

You can ask five different attorneys how they charge for a Probate and you may get five completely different answers. Where families get taken advantage of is when there is not a crystal clear discussion regarding attorney fees at the outset.

I knew a woman once who, after her husband died, went to see an attorney that she went to church with and asked him to handle her husband's Probate. They did not discuss fees. When he finished months later, he sent her a bill for $35,000. She said she does not speak to this attorney any more even though they go to the same church.

Tip: Always work with an attorney who provides you with a fixed fee quote – in writing – prior to commencing the legal services.

Bottom line: Let's assume that completing the North Carolina Probates – first after the husband dies, and again after the wife dies, costs $15,000 after each death. This means that – if the Probate is avoided by using a revocable living trust – the family will save around $30,000.

## More Savings If You Own Out-Of-State Real Estate

If you live in North Carolina and you own real estate in another state when you die, your heirs will have to go through a Probate in North Carolina, and they will also have to go through an "ancillary probate" in the other state. The North Carolina Probate transfers your North Carolina real estate and all other non-real estate assets. The North Carolina Probate does not transfer out-of-state real estate. A probate in that other state must occur to transfer that property to your heirs.

If you have a revocable living trust and you transfer your out-of-state real estate to your trust, this ancillary probate will be avoided.

### Living Trust Settlement Faster than Probate

**Example.** Dad died owning two investment accounts. Each account held about $300,000 of investments. One account was titled in Dad's name. The other account was titled in the name of Dad's revocable living trust. After Dad died, the successor trustee of Dad's trust was given immediate access to the trust account and within one week was able to distribute the account to Dad's beneficiaries. The account that was titled in Dad's name, however, had to go through a Probate with the family incurring thousands in costs and it taking several months for the Probate paperwork to make its way through courthouse, and the legal department of the institution which held Dad's account.

Let's look at a typical example of the mechanics of a revocable living trust and how it should work in North Carolina. Let's say you are married and you have three children. You feel it would be in your and your family's best interest to form a revocable living trust. Here's what happens next.

You work with an attorney (hopefully an attorney knowledgeable in living trusts and hopefully someone you have good rapport with) to prepare your revocable living trust. A complete revocable living trust estate plan will also include a last will and testament for you and your spouse, a durable power of attorney, a health care power of attorney, and a living will, and perhaps legal documents transferring your North Carolina real estate to your trust. Once all these documents are prepared, you sign them.

Next, you must fund the trust. You will avoid probate only if all of your "probate assets" have been transferred to your trust before your death. Documents are prepared and signed whereby you and your spouse transfer title to your home, other real estate, stock, bonds, brokerage accounts and mineral interests to your trust. The real estate transfers must be recorded in the public records of the county where the property is located.

### Which assets do not need to be transferred to your revocable living trust?

It's likely that you own assets that do not need to be transferred to your trust – and probate can still be avoided.

IRAs, 401(k) accounts, annuities and life insurance have designated beneficiaries. By their nature, these types of accounts avoid probate. As long as you properly designate beneficiaries, these assets will not be part of your "probate estate" when you die and your beneficiaries will not be required to go through Probate when you die to obtain ownership of these funds.

**Example**. Dad owns an IRA. He names Mom as the primary beneficiary, and he names his two children as equal contingent beneficiaries. When Dad dies, Mom obtains a death certificate and presents it to the financial institution where Dad's IRA is held. Dad's IRA will be transferred into Mom's IRA without a court proceeding.

Do vehicles need to be transferred to my revocable living trust?

There is an easier way. Dad may have a revocable living trust so that his wife and children avoid probate. However, as long as Dad has his Last Will set up correctly, Dad can keep his vehicles in his name and his family will avoid probate.

The North Carolina Department of Motor Vehicles will transfer title of a vehicle after death if a copy of a Will is produced after the death of the owner.

**Example.** Dad owns three vehicles. Dad has a living trust which owns his real estate and his non-IRA investments. Dad leaves his vehicles in his own name but when Dad has his trust prepared he also has a Will prepared leaving his vehicles to Mom. After Dad dies, Mom produces a copy of Dad's Will to the Office of Motor Vehicles and they will re-title the vehicles into Mom's name without needing any Probate court orders.

## Do you need to transfer your bank accounts to your revocable living trust?

There are two schools of thought on whether you should transfer your bank accounts to your revocable living trust if your goal is to avoid the North Carolina Probate.

You can go to your bank and set up new trust bank accounts. You will close your accounts that are in your name and operate out of the new trust accounts. This may be cumbersome, particularly if you have several automatic deposits and withdrawals that must be changed to the new account.

Or, if you want to make it simpler, leave your bank accounts in your name, but take your successor trustee (or some other trusted person) to your bank and set up your existing accounts so that you name someone else as having signature authority on your bank accounts. Now, when you die (or when you and your spouse die), the person you gave signature authority to will have the ability to access your accounts to pay for your funeral, pay other expenses, and close your account to divide the money among the beneficiaries of your revocable living trust.

## What happens to a revocable living trust when the first spouse dies?

How your trust works after the first spouse dies (if you are married and you and your spouse set up a trust) depends on how you set up the trust in the first place.

You could have set up your trust so that the entire trust is now controlled by the surviving spouse, and the surviving spouse can revoke or change any provisions of the entire trust.

Or, you could have set up your trust so that when one spouse dies, that spouse's share of the trust becomes irrevocable. This protects the beneficiaries of the first spouse to die.

**Example.** Dad dies after Dad and Mom created a revocable living trust. Dad has three of his own children from his first marriage. Mom has two children from a prior marriage. When Dad dies, their joint trust assets total $1 million in value. Dad's part of the trust ($500,000) becomes irrevocable. Mom can do whatever she wants with her half, and she continues to be the trustee of Dad's half. She can spend Dad's half if she needs it, but whatever is left in Dad's half when Mom later dies must go to Dad's three children. Also, the assets in the "Dad Trust" will not be included in Mom's estate for federal estate tax purposes.

When the surviving spouse dies, the successor trustee (likely your adult child) will be responsible for following the instructions you gave them in the trust for perhaps terminating the trust, and distributing trust assets to the beneficiaries. If the surviving spouse, at the time of his or her death, owns shares of stock, real estate, or other "probate assets" in his or name (as opposed to owned by the trust) Probate will be necessary to transfer the asset out of the decedent's name to the trust pursuant to the "pour-over Will." If the trust was funded properly the "pour-over Will" may never need to be used.

## The following are important points about revocable living trusts in North Carolina:

(1)    Taxes. Typically you and your family will pay no more or less taxes if you have a revocable living trust. All trust income flows through the trust to you personally. The trust pays no tax;

(2)    Funding. It is important that you transfer assets to your trust during your lifetime. Typical assets you must transfer to your trust include your real estate (both in North Carolina and out of state), mineral interests, stocks, bonds and mutual funds;

(3)    Assets You Can Keep in Your Name. Keep your IRAs, 401(k)s, annuities and life insurance in your name, but designate beneficiaries on a designated beneficiary form.

(4)    Save Time and Estate Settlement Costs. The probate procedure in the State of North Carolina takes months, if not years. Using a revocable living trust to avoid a North Carolina Probate can save your loved ones the cost, stress and inherent delays involved in a Probate.

(5)    Work with an expert. North Carolina has its own trust code which is different from all other state trust codes. The trust laws change annually. Make sure you work with a North Carolina attorney that is familiar with the nuances of the North Carolina trust and Probate law.

**The following people typically are eager to establish a revocable living trust in North Carolina:**

(1)    You have been through a difficult North Carolina Probate or an out of state probate in the past – perhaps when your parents died – and you don't want to put your loved ones through the same thing.

(2)    Perhaps your parents had a revocable living trust when they died, and you saw how easy it was to settle their estate.

(3)    You don't want your spouse or children to go through an expensive, timely, stressful, and public court process when you die.

(4)    You live in North Carolina but you own real estate in other states. A revocable living trust will avoid the North Carolina Probate and the ancillary probate in those other states where you own real estate;

(5)    You want someone else to manage your assets for you. You can establish your revocable living trust and name someone else as your trustee (such as a trusted friend, advisor, relative, or a corporate trustee) so that they can handle your investments, bank accounts, and also handle purchases and sales of assets on your behalf.

While the determination of whether you should have a Will-based estate plan or a trust-based estate plan depends on your circumstances and objectives, it is fair to state that your Will based plan is easy to set up but requires court supervision of your estate settlement, while a trust based plan requires you to transfer assets to your trust during your lifetime but avoids court interference when you die.

## Other Uses For Trusts
## Trusts for Minors

If you have minor children, or if you plan on leaving a bequest to your young grandchildren, you should consider a trust.

In North Carolina, if a minor (a child under the age of 18) inherits in his or her own name, then a court-supervised guardianship proceeding is necessary. The court will appoint a guardian to oversee the minor's inheritance, and any payments to or on behalf of the minor must be approved by the court. This is an expensive and cumbersome proceeding.

If you have minor children, you should designate in your Will that any inheritance your children receive will be placed in trust so that the trustee that you name can manage the assets and use it for the right reasons without having to get the courts involved.

If you would like to leave a bequest to your grandchildren, you should do the same, particularly if your grandchildren are young and unable to manage an inheritance for themselves.

**Example.** Grandma and Grandpa want to leave $50,000 to each of their five grandchildren (who currently range in age from 15 down to 2). If the grandchildren inherit this money while they are minors, a guardianship proceeding will be required in which the court will appoint a guardian to oversee the funds. If the money needs to be used prior to the grandchild's 18th birthday, a judge must approve the expenditure. At the grandchild's 18th birthday, the guardian must turn the funds over to the grandchild.

A better alternative is to provide in the last will and testament of Grandma and Grandpa that these funds for the grandchildren will be placed in trust after the death of Grandma and Grandpa. Perhaps each grandchild's parents could be the trustees of the trust, and Grandma and Grandpa would authorize the trustees to use the funds for the grandchild's health, education and welfare. Perhaps Grandma and Grandpa could also provide that whatever funds remained in the trust when the grandchild reached the age of 25 (or some other age when it is more likely that the grandchild would have matured) would be turned over to the grandchild.

### Trusts to avoid estate taxes

The federal estate tax exemption has increased in recent years from $600,000 to $5,340,000. Less than 1% of families are subject to the federal estate tax. However, for those families that are subject to this tax, it can be devastating.

Many individuals and couples who are facing a federal estate tax at their deaths transfer assets to an irrevocable trust during their lifetime to remove those assets from their estate. Each person can transfer $14,000 each year either to an individual or to a trust for the benefit of that individual.

**Example.** Mom and Dad have a combined estate of $13,000,000. Even with a properly drafted will or revocable living trust, there will be an estate tax bill due to the IRS of about $1,000,000 after the death of the surviving spouse.

They have three children and seven grandchildren. Since both Mom and Dad can transfer $14,000 to an unlimited number of people each year tax free, they decide to create an irrevocable trust for the benefit of their children and grandchildren, and they transfer assets valued at $280,000 each year to the trust. They name their trusting son as the trustee of the trust. It will be his job to manage the trust assets until Mom and Dad die, and then distribute the trust assets in accordance with the instructions given him by the trust instrument.

## Special Needs Trusts

Individuals with certain disabilities can receive cash benefits and medical coverage from various government programs. In order to qualify for these benefits, the individual's income and resources must not exceed certain levels.

If a parent leaves a bequest to a special needs child, the inherited assets may preclude the child from receiving the benefits. The government, however, has established rules to allow assets to be held in trust for the benefit of a special needs child, preserving the government benefits, as long as certain parameters are met.

These trusts, called Special Needs Trusts, preserve government benefit eligibility and leave assets that will meet certain needs of a special needs individual. Special Needs Trusts are typically designed so that the trust assets can be used to supplement, not supplant, government benefits. Trust assets are typically distributed to third parties to pay for items other than the food and shelter of the disabled individual.

## Trusts for Married Couples

Trusts are commonly used by married couples. Many married couples would like for the surviving spouse to benefit from the assets accumulated during the lifetime of the couple, but married people don't like the idea of all of their assets going to the surviving spouse's "new" spouse.

**Example:** Ted and Angela have $1,000,000 in assets. These assets are joint property because they were accumulated during their marriage. Ted has two children from a prior marriage. Angela has one child from her prior marriage. Ted wants Angela to have access to their estate if he dies first, but he fears that it will all be left to Angela's "new" husband if Angela marries after Ted's death. Or, if Angela does not remarry, she might leave the entire estate to her one child when she dies—to the exclusion of Ted's children. So, Ted establishes a trust (this trust can be in his will or it can be a stand alone trust) so that Ted's share of the property goes to the trust when Ted dies. Angela will be able to use the trust property after Ted dies for her health, education, maintenance and support. When Angela dies, the remaining trust assets will revert back to Ted's children.

## Charitable Trusts

You can donate assets to charity during your lifetime. You can also leave assets to a charity when you die by naming them in your Will or on your beneficiary designation forms.

If you donate assets to a charity while you are alive, you may benefit from a charitable income tax deduction, but you will receive no further financial benefit.

If you leave assets to a charity when you die, your estate is entitled to a charitable estate tax deduction, but you get no tax or other financial benefits while you are alive.

If you create a charitable remainder trust during your lifetime and transfer assets to it, you will receive a charitable income tax deduction when you transfer assets to the trust, and the trust, within certain parameters, will pay you an income for the rest of your lifetime or for a certain period of years. Since the trust is a "charitable" trust, it can sell the assets that you transferred to it without incurring any capital gains tax on the appreciation. At your death or at the end of a term, the assets are transferred to your favorite charity or charities.

## Conclusion

While trusts can be confusing at first to the lay person, trusts can be a valuable estate planning tool. Common types of trusts in North Carolina include:

- Revocable living trusts. Becoming increasingly popular for North Carolina residents because it allows families to avoid the court-supervised Probate procedure at death and provides for a faster and less-costly estate settlement at death. A revocable living trust can be extra beneficial if you own real estate in other states allowing your family to avoid multiple probates

- Trusts for minors. If there's a chance your minor child or minor grandchild will inherit assets from you, then you need to make sure those assets will be placed in trust so the courts won't need to supervise the minor's assets and so that the minor will be protected from squandering the assets when he or she reaches the age of 18.

- Trusts to avoid estate tax. Not as popular now since the estate tax exemption has increased from $600,000 to $5,340,000, but if estate taxes are likely, you need to consider these irrevocable trusts.

- Special Needs Trust. If you have a child with special needs, make sure any inheritance you leave that child is placed in a Special Needs Trust. This will help preserve government benefits that benefit the child.

- Trusts for Married Couples. A way to make your assets available for your spouse after you die, but when your spouse later dies, the trust assets will revert back to your heirs, not your spouse's heirs.

- Charitable Trust. A vehicle which allows you to transfer appreciated assets to a charity, have them sold with no tax consequences, receive an income off those assets for your lifetime, and at your death the remaining trust assets are passed along to your favorite charity.

# CHAPTER 6

# MULTIPLE MARRIAGES
## Protect your second spouse AND your children from your first marriage

The North Carolina property laws work well for most traditional North Carolina families. The husband and wife have children. After both the husband and wife die, their combined assets are typically divided equally among their children. It can be pretty cut and dried.

We now live in a society where it's "normal" for people to get married two or more times. It's not uncommon, and often encouraged, for surviving spouses to remarry after the death of their first spouse. Many people get a divorce and then marry someone else.

Proper estate planning is critical in multiple marriage situations – particularly when each spouse has children from a prior marriage.

## Typical Example Which Excludes the Children

Larry and Martha get married at age 60. They each have two adult children from their prior marriages. Larry wants to provide for both his new wife and his two children. He writes a Will leaving everything he owns to his wife. He also stipulates that if Martha dies before him, he wants everything he owns to go to his two children when he dies. Martha also writes her will with similar provisions. Larry dies and all his assets go to Martha. When Martha dies five years later, she leaves everything she owns to her two children. Larry's two children get nothing.

## Common Example Minimizing Care of the Spouse

Steve and Dot get married at age 60. Steve brings into the marriage assets worth $1,000,000, including the home Steve and Dot live in. Dot's assets are less than $100,000. Steve has three children from his prior marriage. Steve wants to provide for Dot and his three children when he dies, but he doesn't get his affairs in order. When Steve dies unexpectedly, most of Steve's assets, including two-thirds of the home and other assets Steve brought into the marriage (these assets are his separate property because he brought them into the marriage) are transferred to Steve's three children under the intestate laws. If any of the children wish, they can force Dot pay them for their share of the home. Dot also will have less than one-half of the cash and other assets of Steve for her support in the future.

Much of the bickering that takes place over an inheritance occurs when children and their step-parent fight over a deceased's assets. The relationship that a child has with his or her step-parent, in general, is often not as strong as the relationship a child has with his or her surviving parent.

## Separate Property Rules Confuse the Uninformed

Married people often mistakenly believe that if they each keep their accounts in their own name, they will avoid problems upon a death or divorce because they each have their own accounts. North Carolina property laws, however, don't work that way.

**Since this book is about Estate Planning and not Divorce Planning, only a little mention of general divorce law will be made here:**

The basic philosophy of the divorce courts in North Carolina is that marriage is many things, including an economic partnership. What is earned during the marriage, no matter by who, and no matter whose name it is held in, should usually be split equally upon divorce. Hence the confusion with true "community property" states.

**Example:** George and Debbie married each other, the second marriage for each. Each has children by the first marriage. George has a beautiful home they move into, and he also has a business and $500,000 in a brokerage account. Debbie has her own home, which she sells for $200,000, and puts those funds into a joint brokerage account with George. Over the course of the marriage, George earns $250,000, which he puts into his brokerage account.

Upon divorce, assets subject to division by the court would include the joint brokerage account and George's home. By using his home as the joint residence, George made it a joint asset of the marriage, subject to the jurisdiction of the Family Court. George's brokerage account is now subject to court division, also, since he deposited $250,000 in assets earned during the marriage into an otherwise separate property account. No doubt the divorce lawyers will fight about this account.

However, if George dies, and his will says all of his property goes to his children, the house and brokerage account go to them, along with one-half of the joint brokerage account. Debbie doesn't even end up with as much as she began the marriage with.

### Last Will and Testament

Big mistakes are often made when married persons, particularly those who have children from a previous marriage, leave all of their assets to their current spouse in their Will.

**Example.** Jude and Laura are each married for the second time. They each have two children from their prior marriages. Jude wants to provide for his new wife so he signs a Will leaving all of his property to Laura. He "trusts" that Laura will leave a substantial bequest to Jude's children. When Jude dies, all of his assets are put in Laura's name. Jude's adult children get nothing. Laura's Will now provides that everything she owns when she dies goes to Laura's two children. When Laura dies, Jude's children get nothing.

There are basically three ways that a married person can protect his children from a previous marriage:

1. Leave bequests to your children directly, even if you die before your spouse does;
2. Leave your spouse a life estate in your property and give your children the remainder;
3. Leave your assets in trust for the benefit of your spouse and your children.

### Bequests To Children Directly

Even if you are married, you can bequeath assets directly to your children if you want to make sure that they inherit from you.

**Example.** Dan and Carol are married. They are each in their second marriage and they are each 70 years old. Dan has two condos and stock that he wants his children to inherit. Dan provides in his Last Will and Testament that he wants his four children to inherit these condos and this stock. When he dies, these assets get transferred directly to his four children.

While money is no easier to talk about at age 70 than it is at age 30, seniors, especially, should understand and discuss their estate options before getting married. Otherwise, Carol could, literally, be left out in the cold.

## Bequeath a Life Estate to Your Spouse and the Remainder to Your Children

Sometimes, a client suggests leaving the surviving second spouse a Life Estate in the marital home, with the remainder to children of a prior marriage. A Life Estate is the right to the exclusive use of an asset for the remainder of the Life Estate holder's life with the remainder going to, usually, children of a prior marriage. If you are married and you have children from a previous spouse, you may want to bequeath your current spouse a Life Estate in your home or other real property. But, Life Estates can be tricky to manage.

Usually, a life estate is only in real estate, with the cash and other personal property given outright to the surviving spouse or to other heirs. The only time this arrangement comes close to working adequately, is if the surviving spouse gets all of the personal property and a life estate in the only piece of property of the marriage, namely the marital residence. This way there is some chance of passing a small inheritance on to the children.

**Example.** Dan leaves Carol a life estate in the marital home, which was in his name alone, as well as leaving her most of his cash and other assets outright. When Carol dies, the house goes to Dan's children, who he has named as remaindermen. Carol may or may not leave Dan's children anything remaining from the assets he left her.

## Bequeath Assets In Trust for Your Spouse and Children

If you want to provide for your spouse and your children, particularly when your spouse is not the parent of your children, you may want to structure your Will so that assets are left in trust for them after your death.

**Example.** Instead of leaving Carol a life estate in his home, and an outright bequest of stock, and cash, Dan leaves them in trust for Carol and his four children from his first marriage. He names Carol as the income beneficiary of the trust for the rest of her lifetime, he names his four children as equal principal beneficiaries of the trust, and Dan names his son, Jimmy, as the trustee of the trust. When Dan dies, all of his assets are re-titled into the name of Jimmy as trustee of the trust. Jimmy must see to it that all of the income, such as dividends and interest, are paid to Carol, and he is authorized to distribute to Carol enough principal to pay for her health, education, maintenance and support. The trust also contains directions regarding payment of repairs, taxes and insurance on the marital home. When Carol dies, the remaining trust assets are divided among Dan's four children.

## Beneficiary Designations

If you have assets in an Individual Retirement Account (IRA) or a 401(k), or if you own life insurance or an annuity, you need to make certain that the beneficiary designations are set up properly – especially if you are married and you have children from a prior marriage.

**Example.** Joe retired from the local chemical plant after 30 years of employment. When he retired, he rolled his 401(k) into an IRA. In his Will, he left one-half of his IRA to Elaine, and the other half to his children. Joe wanted to provide for both his current wife and his children. However, he named Elaine as the beneficiary of his IRA. His IRA, valued at $600,000 was his largest asset in value. When he died, his entire IRA went to Elaine. Elaine then rolled the IRA into an IRA in her name only and named her three children as the beneficiaries to receive the IRA at her death. When Elaine died, her children (not Joe's children) received the entire IRA.

To protect both his wife and children, Joe could have done one of two things with the beneficiary designation of his IRA:

1. Designate his wife as beneficiary of part of his IRA (let's

say 50%) and designate his children as beneficiaries of the other 50%. Some financial institutions require that your spouse consent in writing when you name someone other than your spouse as the primary beneficiary of your IRA; or

2. Designate a trust as the beneficiary of your IRA, so your spouse can benefit from the trust while he or she is alive, but at your surviving spouse's death, the trust assets (the IRA) go to your children (and not to whomever your spouse may designate).

## Conclusion

If you or your spouse has been married more than once:

- Avoid the trap of your separate property turning into joint property
- Avoid the trap of thinking that you will always have the use of an asset because you share it now with your spouse
- Take advantage of trusts to provide for your spouse and your children
- Use caution when designating beneficiaries of retirement plans, life insurance and annuities

# CHAPTER 7

# DEATH AND TAXES
## Benjamin Franklin said it best

Everyone wants to avoid taxes. When many people think about avoiding taxes, they think about avoiding income tax. North Carolina residents have to be concerned with several types of taxes when they are planning their estates. Some of the taxes that can be minimized include the Federal estate tax, the income tax, the capital gains tax, and the property tax.

## The North Carolina Inheritance Tax is Gone

For many years, heirs owed the State of North Carolina an inheritance tax based on the value of their inheritance. The inheritance tax rate was based on the value of the inheritance and the relationship between the deceased and the heir.

The North Carolina Inheritance Tax is dead and gone. It was eliminated effective January 1, 2013

## Federal Estate Tax

The federal estate tax applies to estates of people who were residents in any of the 50 states. When it applies, it is significant. Essentially, when a person dies, we have to add up the fair market value (as determined by appraisal or otherwise) of everything the deceased owned – their house, cars, bank accounts, IRAs, 401(k)s, life insurance, stock, businesses they own, other real estate, and much more – and if the value of those assets exceed an exemption amount ($5,340,000 for deaths occurring in 2014) there may be federal estate tax due on the amount in excess of the exemption. The taxed portion will be taxed at a rate of about 40%.

For many years the estate tax exemption was $600,000 and many more estates were subject to the federal estate tax. As the exemption has increased to $5,340,000, it has decreased the number of families and estates subject to the tax.

## Future of the Estate Tax

In December 2010, sweeping new federal estate tax laws were passed. However, the new tax laws that were passed at that time were only put into effect until December 31, 2012. Since Congress and the President passed new tax laws in January, 2013, the exemption amount is $5,340,000 for deaths occurring in 2014, and the estate tax rate is 40%.

## Using Deceased Spouse's Unused Exclusion Amount

Under pre-2010 federal estate tax law, each spouse had an estate tax exemption. If the estate of the first spouse to die did not use his or her exemption, it would be lost and the surviving spouse could not use any of the exemption of the first spouse to die. This all changed in 2011, and the new tax act passed in January, 2013 kept portability in place

Now we have something called "portability." It allows the surviving spouse to increase his or her exemption amount by the amount of the unused exemption amount of the deceased spouse who died after 2010.

**Example.** Dad died in 2011 with an estate of $2,000,000. His estate was not large enough to fully utilize the $5,000,000 exemption. Assuming an election was made by the Dad's executor, Mom's estate tax exemption will be $8 million ($5 million plus the $3 million that Dad's estate did not use).

Note that in order for the surviving spouse to increase his or her exemption amount, the executor of the deceased spouse's estate must make an election on the first spouse's timely filed estate tax return.

## Calculating Federal Estate Tax

Essentially, when a person dies, the executor is responsible for determining the total value of the assets that the deceased owned on the date of his or her death. If the gross value of the assets exceeds the exemption amount, a federal estate tax return must be filed by the executor within nine months after the death.

The estate tax return is complicated to most people. If the deceased owned a business, a home or other real estate, appraisals must be obtained and attached to the return.

All of the investments and financial accounts must be reviewed to determine date of death values, and those values must be listed on the return.

The estate is entitled to deduct certain items before calculating the net estate. Common deductions include debts the deceased owed on the date of death, costs to administer the estate, bequests to a surviving spouse, and bequests to charitable organizations.

**Example**. Ralph died on January 15, 2011. He and his wife Theresa together owned a home worth $1,500,000, a joint investment account valued at $6,500,000, an office condominium, in Ralph's name alone, worth $2,000,000, and miscellaneous other assets such as vehicles and bank accounts in Ralph's name, totaling $500,000. The total value of Ralph's property was: one-half of the house ($750,000) plus one-half of the investment account ($3,250,000) plus the office condo ($2,000,000) plus all of the miscellaneous assets ($500,000). This totals $6,500,000. So, Ralph's gross estate was 6,500,000. In Ralph's Will, he left his half of the home ($750,000) and condominium ($1,000,000) to his wife, Theresa, and he left everything else he owned to his children. Since his estate received a $1,750,000 deduction for the bequests to his surviving spouse, Ralph's net estate was valued at $4,750,000, and no federal estate tax was due

.

## How to Avoid Capital Gains Tax

Most people, when they think about avoiding taxes at death, think about how to avoid the federal estate tax. With the estate tax exemption at $5 million ($10 million for married couples), most families do not have to be concerned about paying federal estate tax.

The tax that often creeps up and bites people is the capital gains tax. Capital gains tax is paid when you sell an asset that has appreciated in value. For example, if you buy stock for $20,000 and later sell the stock for $100,000, you will have $80,000 of capital gain and you must pay tax on this gain.

## Step Up in Basis

When you die, the basis of your assets will be "stepped up." Your heirs will get a new basis. Your heirs' basis will not be what you paid for the asset. Your heirs' basis will be the fair market value of the asset on the date that you died, which is the value used to compute how large your estate is for

Federal inheritance purposes.

**Example.** Years ago, Jane bought stock in XYZ Company for $50,000. When Jane died many years later the stock was worth $400,000. Jane left this stock equally to her two children so that each child received stock that was worth $200,000. Since the basis of the stock was stepped up at death, each child will have a capital gains basis of $200,000 on their share of the stock. If they sell the stock for $200,000 shortly after Jane dies, they will incur no capital gains tax as a result of the sale.

## Carry Over Basis

Note that this basis rule is different if you donate appreciated assets during your lifetime. The donee does not receive a step up in basis on stock that is given to him or her during the donor's lifetime. If, in the previous example, Jane had given the stock to her two children just prior to Jane's death, the children would each have a basis of $25,000 on their share of the stock and they would have incurred significant capital gains tax on a subsequent sale of the stock – even if they waited until after Jane died to sell the stock.

For this reason, many people choose to "hold on" to their appreciated assets and let their heirs inherit them at the stepped-up basis, rather than giving appreciated assets to heirs during life causing donees to have a carry-over basis.

## Married Couples and the Capital Gains Tax

How married couples structure their bequests to each other and to their family can have a significant impact on how much capital gains tax heirs will have to pay when appreciated assets are later sold. And the fact that there is so much uncertainty about future estate tax does not make these decisions any easier.

For starters, be aware of the rule in North Carolina, that when the first spouse dies, only the decedent's share of joint property receives a step-up in basis to the value as of the date of death. When the surviving spouse later dies, assets "owned" by the surviving spouse get stepped-up again.

**Example.** Richard and Marie have $1 million of jointly owned property. Richard died leaving his entire estate to Marie. All of Richard's one-half interest in the property receives a step-up in basis when Richard dies. Marie dies years later when these assets are valued at $2 million. Because Richard left it all to Marie and Marie "owned" it all at her death, their children will enjoy another step-up in basis on all the family assets. If Richard had left Marie only a life estate in his estate (that is, the right to use the assets while Marie's was alive, with the remainder going to someone else), then only Marie's half of the assets would receive a step-up when she died because she did not "own" what was formerly

Richard's half.

Bottom line on capital gains tax: Don't forget about potential capital gains tax when planning your estate – it often gets overlooked. Structuring your bequests the wrong way can cost your family hundreds of thousands (or more) of unnecessary capital gains tax.

## How Married Couples Avoid Estate Tax

There are many estate tax planning techniques that individuals and married couples can utilize. One of those techniques is to have the Will or trust set up properly to make certain that each married person's estate utilizes its maximum estate tax exemption. This allows married couples who die in 2014 to exempt $10,680,000 from the federal estate tax, because each estate is entitled to a $5,340,000 exemption – but you have to have things set up just right.

The most common way couples arrange their Wills to avoid estate tax by leaving your estate in a QTIP trust for the benefit of your surviving spouse.

## Avoiding Estate Tax By Using QTIP Trusts

The most common way North Carolina married couples avoid or minimize federal estate tax is to provide that at the first spouse's death, the first spouse's assets remain in trust for the surviving spouse's lifetime. If the trust language provides that the surviving spouse is entitled to the income for the trust assets for the rest of her lifetime, then estate tax can be avoided at the first death.

QTIP stands for qualified terminable interest property. Other terms often used in conjunction with this type of trust include credit shelter trust, bypass trust, marital deduction trust, and QTIP trust. The terms of these trusts can be spelled out in the deceased's revocable living trust or in the deceased's last will and testament.

## Gifts of $14,000

You may have heard that you can donate or give $14,000 (it used to be $10,000) to people each year without tax consequences. Many people are confused by this rule.

Typically no one pays income tax on a gift regardless of the value of the gift. A sizable gift, however, will have gift and estate tax consequences.

**Example.** Alice gives her daughter, Suzanne, $114,000 on February 1, 2014, to help Suzanne buy a home. This gift has no income tax effect on either Alice or her daughter, Suzanne. No tax is due as a result of the gift. Gifts of $14,000 or less each calendar year need not be reported, but the fact that Alice gave $114,000 to Suzanne must be reported on a federal gift tax return (IRS Form 709), showing that Alice has used

$100,000 of her $5,340,000 federal estate tax exemption. If Alice dies in 2014, her estate tax exemption (the amount exempt from federal estate tax) will be $5,240,000 instead of $5,340,000 because she used part of her estate tax exemption during her lifetime.

Many people who make gifts to others in excess of $14,000 in a calendar year do not have an estate that exceeds the applicable estate tax exemption of $5,340,000. So there really is no tax consequence at all to making large gifts, other than the requirement of filing a federal gift tax return disclosing that the gift was made.

## Legal Tax Avoidance Techniques

Much has been said and written about avoiding federal estate tax and other taxes at death. The increase in the estate tax exemption to $5,340,000 will exclude many estates from being subject to the tax. However, for those families that are still subject to the estate tax, the following are popular estate tax planning tools:

1. Prepare Your Will or Trust Properly. For many people (especially married couples), having your Last Will and Testament or Revocable Living Trust conform to the estate tax laws will avoid estate tax completely. This allows married couples to exempt up to $10,680,000 from estate tax.

2. Annual gifts. You can give away $14,000 to as many people as you want, every year, to reduce your estate. If you have four children and eight grandchildren, you could (if you wanted to) reduce your taxable estate by $168,000 each year by making $14,000 gifts to each of them.

3. Use Life Insurance To Pay Estate Tax. This is a tool made popular by the life insurance industry. You are not reducing your estate tax by purchasing life insurance, but you are making gifts to children or others and the gifted money is used to purchase life insurance on your life that might pay the estate tax liability when you die.

4. Capital Gains Tax. Don't put appreciated assets in your kids' names without first considering the capital gains tax effect. Your heirs will enjoy the step-up in basis only if they inherit assets from you when you die, not if you give assets to them during your lifetime.

5. Gifts and Bequests To Charity. What you leave to a qualified charity completely avoids estate tax. If Bill Gates and his wife leave their entire estate to their charitable foundation (or any other charity) no estate tax will be due at their deaths. There are many ways to donate or bequeath money to charity – some simple and some complex.

**Conclusion**

You can't avoid death, but you may be able to minimize or

avoid death tax by:

- Making sure your estate utilizes its $5,340,000 exemption available for deaths occurring in 2014
- Properly setting up—if you are married—your Will or your Revocable Living Trust so there will be no tax upon the death of the first spouse regardless of the size of the estate
- Ensuring that your heirs receive a step-up in basis – not just hen the first spouse dies but again when the surviving spouse dies
- Utilizing annual exclusion gifts of $14,000 during your lifetime to reduce your taxable estate at your death

# CHAPTER 8

# LIVING WILLS
## Making your wishes known about life support machines

You have the right to control decisions relating to your own medical care, including the decision to have life-sustaining procedures withheld or withdrawn in instances where you are diagnosed as having a terminal and irreversible condition, are unconscious and most probably will never regain consciousness, or suffer from advanced dementia that is most likely not reversible.

The North Carolina legislature has determined that the artificial prolongation of life for a person diagnosed as having any of these three types of conditions may cause loss of individual and personal dignity, which secures a burdensome existence while providing nothing medically necessary or beneficial to the person.

It's difficult to make a decision to authorize the withdrawal of life support machines for someone you love. The purpose of our living will laws is to allow you to tell your family and your doctors what your wishes are regarding life support machines, so that your family does not have to make that final decision. You've made your decision for them in advance by signing your living will.

Your Health Care Agent (who you appointed in your Health Care Power of Attorney) will most likely have to make this ugly decision for you, because you won't be able to communicate you rational decision at that time. Without a Living Will (also known as an Advance Health Care Directive) from you, then no matter what decision your Agent makes, there will be someone in the family who will forever after think your Agent made the wrong decision.

## Making a Living Will

You may make, at any time, a written living will which directs the withholding or withdrawal of life-sustaining procedures, that becomes effective if you have any of these three irreversible conditions.

The North Carolina Legislature has created a sample form for a living will. You are not required to use the State sample living will form, but, if you create your own, you need to insure that it meets the requirements for witnessing and execution. Note also that the North Carolina form is not guaranteed to be accepted in any other State, due to either language requirements or execution requirements, or both.

## PARTS OF THE NORTH CAROLINA LIVING WILL DOCUMENT

The North Carolina Living Will contains several sections, some simple and some more involved.

I.    The beginning section is simple: it identifies who you are, and states that this Living Will applies if you lack the capacity to communicate your own health care decisions.

II.    Then comes an involved sections, which state that IF you have one of three medical situations:

1.  I have an incurable or irreversible condition that will result in my death within a relatively short period of time; OR,

2.  I become unconscious and my health care providers determine that, to a high degree of medical certainty, I will never regain my consciousness; OR

3.  I suffer from advanced dementia or any other condition which results in the substantial loss of my cognitive ability and my health care providers determine that, to a high degree of medical certainty, this loss is not reversible.

III.    Then you may direct your health care providers to do ONE of the following two options:

1. They MAY withhold or withdraw life-prolonging

measures; or

2. They SHALL withhold or withdraw life-prolonging measures.

**IV.** AND you also get to say if,

1. You want to receive artificial hydration AND artificial nutrition (i.e. through tubes), or
2. You ONLY want to receive artificial hydration (i.e. through tubes); or
3. You ONLY want to receive artificial nutrition (i.e. through tubes).

**V.** AND you also get to say if,

1. Your Health Care Agent MUST follow your directions; or
2. Your Health Care Agent MAY override your directions.

**VI.** Then there are a few more basic provisions that do not

1. require as much thought and discussion: That you want to be kept as comfortable as possible, no matter what;
2. that you understand what you are telling your health care providers to do;
3. that your health care providers may legally rely on this living will;
4. that you want this living will to be effective everywhere; and,
5. language about how you may revoke this living will.

**VII.** Finally, your written living will must be signed by you in the presence of two witnesses. The witnesses must not be related to you by blood or marriage, work for the health care facility where you are a patient or the doctor treating you, and a witness must not be someone who would inherit from you when you die.

## Life-Sustaining Procedure

What is a "life-sustaining procedure?" It's generally defined as any medical procedure or intervention which, within reasonable medical judgment, would serve only to prolong the dying process for a person diagnosed as having a terminal and irreversible condition, including such procedures as the invasive administration of nutrition and hydration and the administration of cardiopulmonary resuscitation. A "life-sustaining procedure" shall not include any measure deemed necessary to provide comfort care.

## Revoking Your Living Will

You may revoke your living will at any time by doing any of the following:

- Destroying your living will or by directing some other person to destroy your living will

- Writing a revocation expressing your intent to revoke your living will. You must sign and date the revocation

- By making an oral or nonverbal expression of your intent to revoke your living will. This type of revocation becomes effective upon communication to your attending physician.

## If No Living Will Exists

It is common for people who have never signed a living will to enter a terminal and irreversible condition. When this occurs, the following individuals usually have priority to make the decision, in the following order:

1. The court appointed legal guardian of the patient, if one has been appointed
2. The patient's spouse.
3. An adult child of the patient.
4. The parents of the patient.
5. The patient's sibling.
6. The patient's other ascendants or descendants.

## Registration of Living Wills in North Carolina

Because keeping track of your Living Will can be an issue, especially as one ages and households are moved and/or downsized, the State of North Carolina has an on-line process to file the properly executed Living Wills with the North Carolina Office of the Secretary of State. By going to this web-site: **http://www.secretary.state.nc.us/ahcdr/** you will find all the information needed to upload and register your Advance Health Care Directive. The fee for doing this is $10.00, at this time. The downside to this process, unfortunately, is that access to the document requires both a User ID and Pass Word. Over time, some of us think it is more likely that we will forget either the User ID or the Pass Word, or both, then that we will misplace the paper copy of the Living Will. A common problems these days.

# CHAPTER 9

# MEDICAID PLANNING
### Avoid Nursing Home Poverty

### What is Medicaid?

Most of the nursing home residents in North Carolina have their stay paid for, all or in part, by Medicaid. The cost of a monthly nursing home stay in North Carolina can vary from city to city but most nursing homes cost about $5,000 each month. If a married couple is in a nursing home, and they are paying for their care and their medicines and other necessary living expenses, they could be paying out more than $10,000 each month.

An extended nursing home stay can wipe out a family's entire life savings in a few months or a few short years. This is why so many people are interested in finding out how they can qualify for Medicaid, which pays this nursing home cost.

In order to qualify for Medicaid, you must meet Medicaid's definition of "poor." There are other requirements as well –

you must be at least 65 years old, blind or disabled, and your income and assets must be limited.

Title XIX of the Social Security Act, enacted by the Social Security Amendments of 1965, provided for grants to states to implement the Medicaid Program. Medicaid is a federal-state entitlement program that pays for medical services on behalf of low-income eligible persons. Medicaid is financed from federal and state funds.

The vast majority of Medicaid spending for long-term care is on nursing homes. However, Medicaid is available to people who need the type of medical care available in a nursing home setting but who can be treated effectively at home or in the community without being placed in a nursing home. However, Medicaid's resources are limited and there are long waiting lists to receive these Home and Community Based Waiver services.

## Medicaid is Not Medicare!

Even though the names sound similar, the programs are very different. Medicare is the health insurance that most people age 65 and older have in the United States. Medicare is designed to cover the expenses that health insurance typically covers, such as doctor's visits, hospital stays, surgery, and lab tests.

## How Does a Single Person (Unmarried) Become Eligible for Medicaid?

To be eligible for Medicaid, you must pass an income test and an asset test. Let's look first at the income test.

The N.C. General Assembly has established income limits, which county departments of social services use in determining eligibility for Medicaid. These limits are based on the number of persons in a family. If the income of the family is more than the amount set by the General Assembly, there will be a deductible. In North Carolina, you generally qualify for Medicaid from an income point of view if your income is less than your cost of care.

**Personal Needs Allowance.** The amount of money from your income that you are allowed to keep each month is called the personal needs allowance. All of your other income, with a few exceptions such as health insurance premiums, must be paid to the nursing home. The nursing home then bills North Carolina's Medicaid program for the shortfall.

**Asset test.** A single applicant can have no more than $2,000 of "countable" assets. Countable assets include cash, bank accounts, certificates of deposit, IRAs, 401(k) accounts, stocks, bonds, lump sum annuities, cash value in life insurance policies, real estate that is not your home, business interests, and other assets that can be converted to cash. Interests in an estate are countable even if the estate has not been opened or the inheritance is refused. Life estates are also countable.

### What assets don't count for Medicaid?

Countable assets, like the ones described above, are assets that count in terms of qualifying for Medicaid. Non-countable assets, also known as excludable assets, do not count. Owning non-countable assets will not affect your Medicaid eligibility.

**Your home property.** By far the biggest non-countable asset that most of us own is our home property. In North Carolina, the home property is property in which you have an ownership interest and that serves as your primary residence. It includes the house or lot which is the usual residence, all contiguous property, and any other buildings on the home property. Property is contiguous to the residence if it is touching the residential property (even corner to corner) and is not separated by property owned by others. Property separated by a public right of way, such as a road, is considered contiguous.

Your home property will be excluded if you are living in your home, or if you are away from your home because of a medical condition, and you are keeping your home available, and you intend to use it as your home when your condition permits. Your home property is also excluded when you are away from your home and your spouse and/or dependent relative lives there.

Your home property is no longer excludable if offered for sale based on your lack of intent to return. A Nursing Facility resident generally cannot establish a new home property while residing in a facility since you would have never lived there and the new residence would not meet the definition of home property.

The value of your home property that is in a state outside of North Carolina is generally a countable asset.

**Household goods and personal effects.** You can exclude the following items, regardless of value: one wedding ring and one engagement ring per individual, along with prosthetic devices, wheelchairs, hospital beds, dialysis machines and other items required by a person's physical condition if they are not used extensively and primarily by the other members of your household.

A general exclusion of up to $2,000 applies to the total equity value of household goods and personal effects other than those excluded regardless of value.

**Vehicles.** One vehicle per household is excluded, regardless of its value, if anyone in the Medicaid applicant's household uses it for transportation. Medicaid assumes that your vehicle is used for transportation unless there is evidence to the contrary. This exclusion even applies to temporarily inoperable vehicles which are expected to be repaired and used for transportation within the next 12 months.

If you own more than one vehicle, the exclusion applies to the car with the greater equity value, regardless of which car is actually used. The equity value of all other vehicles, including inoperable vehicles and antique cars is counted. Medicaid uses the NADA "Blue Book" trade-in value at www.nadaguides.com.

**Burial Contracts, Burial Funds, and Burial Spaces.** A burial contract is countable if it is revocable or salable, and conditions for its liquidation do not present a significant hardship. However, any portion of the burial contract that clearly represents the purchase of burial space may be excludable, and some or all of the remaining value may be excludable as burial funds. A burial contract is not countable if it cannot be revoked and cannot be sold without significant hardship

**Burial Funds.** Funds set aside for the burial expenses of the Medicaid applicant and his/her spouse may be excluded if those funds are clearly designated for your or your spouse's burial expenses. A maximum exclusion of up to $10,000 each in funds set aside is allowed for you and also your spouse. This amount is reduced by the face value of your burial insurance which has no cash value.

**Burial Spaces.** A fully paid burial space or agreement which represents the purchase of a burial space held for your burial, your spouse's burial, or the burial of immediate family is excluded regardless of value.

## What are the rules if you are married?

If you are married and receiving Medicaid benefits, some of your income can be paid to support your spouse.

The income and asset tests are significantly different if one spouse is in the nursing (the "institutionalized spouse") and the other spouse stays at home or in the community (the "community spouse").

One rule that is rarely understood is that the income of the community spouse is never considered in determining eligibility for an institutionalized spouse.

**Example.** Mary Smith is applying for Medicaid. Her husband receives $4,000 of monthly pension and social security income. Mary receives $600 of monthly social security income. Bill's $4,000 of monthly income is not considered in determining Mary's Medicaid eligibility.

A spouse has full ownership of income paid to his name. A spouse has half ownership of income paid in the names of both spouses. And a spouse has pro rata ownership of income paid in the names of either one or both spouses and another individual.

The amount of the institutionalized spouse's income that a community spouse can keep to live on is called the Maintenance Needs Allowance. Here's how it's calculated. Let's say Bill Smith has $2,000 of monthly income and his wife Mary has $1,000 of monthly income. Bill (the institutionalized spouse) is in the nursing home and Mary (the Community Spouse) wants to know if she can keep any of Bill's income.

We start by determining Bill's income ($2,000) and we deduct his personal needs allowance ($60) and we subtract his health insurance premiums ($150). The institutionalized spouse's liability totals $1,790.

Next, we subtract the community spouse's monthly income ($1,000) from the Spouse's Maintenance Needs Allowance ($2,931.00 for the year 2014) to determine how much of Bill's income that Mary can keep. In this case, Mary can keep all of Bill's monthly income, and there is nothing remaining to pay to the nursing home.

## What's the Asset Rule if You Are Married?

If you are single, in order for you to qualify for Medicaid you must have no more than $2,000 of countable assets.

The asset rules are very different for married couples when one spouse is in the nursing home (institutionalized spouse) and one spouse is at home (community spouse).

In North Carolina, as of 2014, a married couple can exclude one-half of all countable assets, with a minimum of $23,448, up to $117,240 (if total assets were $234,480) and the institutionalized spouse can qualify for Medicaid, once they have "spent down" the excess assets. This amount they can keep is called the Community Spouse Resource Allowance. It's defined as the maximum amount of the couple's combined countable resources that may be allocated to the community spouse.

A married couple's countable assets are defined as including the community spouse's assets, the institutionalized spouse's assets, and the couple's shared assets.

**Example.** In addition to their home and car, Bill and Mary Smith have countable assets totaling $175,000. Bill is in the nursing home. We know he can keep $2,000. Mary can keep $87,500. Bill will not qualify for Medicaid at this time because they have $86,500 "too much" in countable assets (i.e. $175,000 – Bill's $2,000 = $173,000 divided by 2 = $86,500). However, the assets that are allocated to the institutionalized spouse that are in excess of $2,000 must be transferred to the community spouse in order for Bill to remain eligible.

### Estate Recovery – Medicaid Can Take Your Home After You Die

The federal government has required the State of North Carolina (and all other states) to establish an estate recovery program. As a result, The Department of Health and Human Services has established an estate recovery program for the purpose of recovering payments made to nursing homes on behalf of Medicaid recipients.

At the time that a North Carolina resident applies for Medicaid, the applicant shall be informed that federal law and regulations mandate estate recovery action by the state and that payments made by Medicaid may be subject to estate recovery.

Recovery can be made only after the death of the patient and his or her spouse. After the patient dies, Medicaid will serve a notice on the family or heirs of Medicaid's action.

**Example.** Bill Smith is in the nursing home and on Medicaid. His wife Mary lives in their home. Bill was eligible for Medicaid because their home was an exempt asset (for purposes of Medicaid eligibility) and they had spent down their asset to the mandated level. During Bill's stay in the nursing home, he spent $150,000 of Medicaid's funds. After both Bill and Mary die, Medicaid can force the home to be sold to be reimbursed for the Medicaid funds they spent for Bill.

## Penalties for Transfers

Mary Jones would qualify for Medicaid except that she has a bank account with $61,000. Mary decides to give her daughter, Jane, a gift of $60,000. After the gift, Mary has only $1,000. Does Mary now qualify for Medicaid? Not a chance.

When you apply for Medicaid, the application asks you to list any transfers or gifts that you have made to an individual or a trust in the last five years (or 60 months).

If a transfer is discovered during this 60 month look-back period, then the applicant is disqualified for Medicaid until the penalty period expires. The penalty period is determined by dividing the value of the transfer by the Average Monthly Cost to Private Patients of Nursing Facility Services. For 2013, North Carolina has determined that the average cost of a nursing home stay is $6,300. So, if Mary made a transfer of $60,000, she would ineligible for Medicaid for 10 months ($60,000 transfer divided by $6,300 average nursing home cost).

## When Does the Penalty Period Start?

For transfers on or after February 8, 2006, the penalty period starts when the individual is in the nursing home, has less than $2,000 of countable resources, and is determined by Medicaid to be eligible except for the occurrence of the transfer.

By now, you probably realize that North Carolina's Medicaid rules are complex. So let's take a look at some of the planning opportunities that are available.

## Qualifying for Medicaid

Every Medicaid applicant's situation is unique. What may work for one person may not work for another. In developing a Medicaid plan, it's important that you work with someone knowledgeable in this complex area. The following are a few of the techniques often employed in assisting people in qualifying for Medicaid.

The reason that most people fail to qualify for Medicaid is that they have too many countable assets. So most of the Medicaid Planning involves timely transfers of countable assets.

## Owning Exempt Assets

Your house and your car are not countable. Certain burial contracts, burial funds and burial spaces are also not countable. By simply transferring countable assets (such as cash) into non-countable assets, you can qualify for Medicaid.

**Example.** Bill and Mary Smith have a home valued at $150,000. There is $51,000 left on their mortgage. They drive an old car worth $2,000, and they've made no funeral arrangements. They have CDs at the bank totaling $90,000, and their checking and savings accounts total $70,000. Mary is entering the nursing home while Bill will stay at home. Mary presently doesn't qualify for Medicaid they have excess assets. Their countable assets actually total $160,000. Bill's Community Spouse Resource Allowance will be $80,000 (i.e. one-half of the total assets of $160,00). But, after they apply for Medicaid, they use $51,000 of their cash to pay off their mortgage, purchase a better car for $20,000, and use $9,000 to prepay their funerals, Mary will qualify for Medicaid.

## Making Gifts

Making gifts to qualify for Medicaid is one of the most misunderstood aspects of Medicaid Planning. If you take the correct action and structure your estate properly and stay out of the nursing home for five years after you set things up, you can protect your entire estate. If, however, you are like many who don't think about Medicaid eligibility planning until just before a family member goes in the nursing home, you can still take certain actions to protect roughly half of your countable resources.

## Planning in Advance

If you transfer your countable resources out of your name at least five years before you go into a nursing home, you can protect all of your assets. But many people – justifiably so – don't want to put all of their assets into the names of their children. But you can keep some control over your assets by placing them into a particular type of irrevocable trust.

## Who Should You Give Your Assets To?

Good question. Your options include your children, a trust, or a combination of the two.

Most families who engage in Medicaid Planning agree up front that the money that is taken out of the parents' names will be "set aside" in an account or accounts for the children. Children informally agree that they will not touch the money until after their parents die, and the children even informally agree that they will spend the money on the parents if necessary.

Unfortunately, things don't always work out as planned. Many times when parents give money to their children, the children end up spending it. Children have many reasons to spend it: they need it for a new truck or boat; they need to pay off credit card debt; they want a new home; they feel they deserve a vacation; they are influenced by their spouse; or, it's just too easy to spend it. The children could also lose the money by getting divorced, getting sued, or owing the IRS or other creditors. The children might also die before the parents and then the family is stuck trying to retrieve the money from the child's heirs.

## Trusts and Medicaid Planning

What is a trust? A trust, as defined by the North Carolina Trust Code, is the relationship resulting from the transfer of title to property to a person to be administered by him as a fiduciary for the benefit of another.

**Example.** Let's say John McCall has four children. John wants to give his children a gift of $100,000, but he doesn't want them to spend it right away. John knows that if he gives $25,000 to each of his four children, at least three of them will spend it within a week or two. John feels that his daughter, Jenny, is responsible though and will act in accordance with John's wishes. So, John establishes the McCall Family Trust and names Jenny as the trustee of the trust. John would like to continue getting the interest from the $100,000 so he names himself as the income beneficiary of the trust. John would like the principal (the $100,000) to be distributed to his children after John's death. Jenny goes to the bank and sets up the McCall Family Trust bank account. Only Jenny has signature authority over this account because she is the sole trustee. John then transfers $100,000 of his money to this trust account. Jenny thereafter, in her capacity as trustee, manages this money for the rest of John's lifetime, seeing to it that John continues to receive the interest as the income beneficiary of the trust, and Jenny distributes the principal to the four children (the principal beneficiaries) after John's death. Had John needed to move into a nursing home five years after setting this up, the $100,000 would not be considered a countable resource of John for Medicaid eligibility purposes.

Trusts are a popular tool in Medicaid Planning because, if established correctly, trusts can permit individuals and married couples to transfer assets out of their name, but retain control of the assets after they are transferred.

Many parents don't want to put their assets in their children's names because bad things can happen after the assets are transferred. Children might spend the assets, they might be influenced adversely by their spouses, children might get divorced and lose the assets, children may have creditor problems or problems with the IRS, children might get sued.

## What If You Don't Have Five Years?

Many people don't even think about qualifying for Medicaid until their loved one is on the doorstep of the nursing home. These people can't wait five years to qualify – they face the prospects of depleting their life savings before the five years runs out.

Special techniques are available which allow you to save half of your countable resources if you are either already in the nursing home or you are going into the nursing home soon. These techniques require working with someone who really understands the ins and outs of transferring assets out of your name and returning assets back to you.

Every few years the Medicaid eligibility rules change making it harder and harder to protect your assets and qualify for Medicaid. With America's population aging, with the cost of care skyrocketing, and with less and less government funds available, it appears that it will be more important in the future to plan in advance for your potential long term care nursing home stay.

# CHAPTER 10

# PROBATE AN ESTATE
### Handling legal matters when a loved one dies

When a loved one dies, there are many things, both legal and personal, that need to be handled. It's a difficult time for many families. An important legal matter that must occur whenever someone dies owning assets in their name is a probate proceeding.

## What is a Probate Proceeding?

A Probate Proceeding (commonly just called "Probate") is the process of transferring assets from the name of the person who died into the names of the appropriate heirs. Most other states often call this process "probate," also.

Families typically think that Probate just involves the family gathering information on what the decedent owned and bringing it to an attorney, with the decedent's Last Will and Testament, if there was one. Then the attorney prepares a few probate documents, a judge signs an order, and that's it.

In North Carolina, that's not even how it starts. It all begins like this:

## Who Is going to be In charge?

Definitions:

If there is no Will, the person in charge of, and responsible for completing, the estate administration, is called the Administrator (if male) or the Administratrix (if female). If there is a Will which names this person, the lucky person is called either the Executor (if male) or the Executrix (if female). Recently there has been a move to use the term Personal Representative to cover both positions and either gender, which is what we will do in this chapter.

## If There is No Will:

If there is no will, there is a priority set by North Carolina Statutes about who has the primary right to be appointed Personal Representative of the estate. The surviving spouse is first, then surviving children, then others. No matter who wants the job, they must file the application, and notice of their application to be Personal Representative must be published in the paper once a week for two weeks. Then, there will be a hearing before the Clerk of Court, who handles probate matters in North Carolina. If there are multiple parties applying to be Personal Representative, this hearing can become contested, ugly and expensive, since each party will have their own attorney. If there are multiple, equal ranked potential applicants (like siblings) those not contesting the appointment of one of them, must submit notarized agreement that the applicant should be appointed.

Once the Personal Representative is selected by the Clerk of Court, the Personal Representative has to file an Initial Inventory listing all of the assets of the decedent, along with the value of each. At the same time, the Personal Representative has to execute his Oath and post a fidelity bond in an amount based on the value of the personal property expected to flow through the estate. The larger the estate, the larger the bond, the more it costs the estate.

## If There is A Will

If there is a Will, and the person named in the Will to serve as Personal Representative applies to serve, then there is no required publication, but this person, on their application to open the estate, has to list the names and mailing address of each heir under the Will. The Clerk will give each beneficiary notice that the proposed Personal Representative has applied, and the beneficiaries may object if they wish. Assuming no one objects, the named Personal Representative is appointed. No bond is required for NC residents, unless the Will requires one.

## Once the Personal Representative is Appointed

Once the Personal Representative is appointed and has

executed an Oath, and posted Bond, if required, the Personal Representative received Letters Testamentary, which declare that the court has officially appointed this person Personal Representative of the estate. The Letters Testamentary, often referred to simply as "Letters," are proof to the world and especially banks, brokerage houses and insurance companies, that this is the person legally allowed to withdraw the decedent's money or other assets, open and close accounts, and in all other respects deal with the debts and assets of the decedent. The Personal Representative also has to submit to the court an Initial Inventory. The Initial Inventory list all of the assets of the decedent, with their values, that the Personal Representative knows about when he takes office.

## Notice to Creditors

Almost immediately after being appointed, the Personal Representative (or the Personal Representative's attorney) will have a Notice of Creditors published in the local paper. This Notice says, essentially, that anyone who has claims against the decedent should present those claims to the Personal Representative within 90 days of the date of first publication, or be unable to collect. It also instructs people who owe money to the decedent to pay it to the Personal Representative. The Personal Representative name and correct mailing address are given so creditors can submit claims. This notice is published once a week for four weeks, but the 90 day claim filing period begins running on the date of first publication.

## Gathering Bills

Although the Personal Representative has published the Notice of Creditors, if the Personal Representative knows of any bills the decedent owned, the Personal Representative must put them into the "to be paid" pile, also.

Example: When John Auten died, his son, George was appointed his Personal Representative. George knew that his father had a cell phone, owed money on his house and car, had three credit cards, and owed money to his neighbor Fred Jones. Because George knew about these creditors, even if they don't file a formal claim within the 90 day period, they still are creditors of the estate and must be paid.

If someone files a claim that the Personal Representative thinks is invalid, Personal Representative can deny the claim. Then the creditor can either give up the claim or have a hearing before the Clerk to prove the validity of the claim. Naturally, the Personal Representative will have the estate attorney representing the estate, trying to show that the claim is not valid. Even small claims can generate large defense costs and legal fees.

## Collecting Assets and Reporting Them

Just as George has to gather all of his father's bills, he also has to discover and collect all assets owned by his father. George should get a Federal Tax ID number for the estate, and open an estate checking account, in order to have somewhere to deposit estate funds that is separate from his own personal checking account. This is the account he will use to pay estate bills from, also.

## Probate vs. Non-probate Assets

The North Carolina Probate Court categorizes the decedent's assets as either "probate" or "non-probate" assets. A probate asset is one which is in the decedent's name when he dies and does not automatically pass to someone else at the instant of death. Examples are:

Probate assets:
- vehicle, boat, trailer titles solely or jointly in the decedent's name;
- bank or brokerage account solely in the decedent's name;
- Stock or bond certificates solely in the decedent's name;
- Promissory Notes or Mortgages solely or jointly in the decedent's name;
- Some Real Estate

A non-probate asset is one which does automatically pass to someone else when the decedent dies, whether or not the decedent had a Will. Examples are:

Non-probate assets:
- Individual Retirement Accounts (IRAs)
- 401(k) accounts
- Life insurance
- Keogh accounts
- 403(b) accounts
- Annuities
- U.S. Savings Bonds titled in the name of the decedent "or" someone else
- Assets titled in the name of a trust

When you open one of these types of accounts with someone else, the fine print in the contract you sign to open the account typically says that this is a Joint and Survivorship Account, which means the survivor automatically inherits everything in the account when the other party dies. This contract agreement overrides anything one of the account owner may put in their Will. The account does not have to be set up this way, but that is the way it automatically happens unless you direct otherwise.

**Example.** John Auten and his wife, Mary, opened a joint checking account at the local bank. When Mary passed away, her Will said her share of this account was to go to her daughter, Sarah. But, John became the sole owner of everything in that account, because the documents signed at the bank to open the account were the standard "joint and survivorship" type. Mary's Will does not control.

Now John wants to put George on a new account, so George can write checks to pay John's bills. But, John, who has three children, doesn't want George to get all of the money in the account automatically. He sets up the account so George is an authorized signer, but his children are the beneficiaries. When John dies, the balance will go into his three children equally.

## Real Estate In North Carolina

### Tenancy by the Entirety

In North Carolina, if title to real estate is held in the names of husband and wife, State law presumes they intended to hold title as Tenants by the Entirety. This means the survivor automatically inherits the decedent's share. If husband and wife do not want to hold title as tenants by the entirety, the Deed to them must clearly state words to the effect of "To be held as Tenants in Common and not as Tenants by the Entirety." "Entireties" property, as it is commonly called, is not includable in the estate. Property owned outright by the decedent or as tenant in common with other parties, in a non-probate asset.

### All Other Real Estate

In North Carolina, when someone dies owning real estate,

either in their name alone or as tenants in common with other owners, their share of the real estate instantly transfers to its new owner. The new owner will be someone in one of two groups: the devisee named in the Will; or, if there is no Will, those who would inherit under the North Carolina Statute of Descent and Distribution (the intestacy laws). Transfer via intestacy is valid immediately. Transfer via Will must go through Probate, to have the Will verified by the court and make it a public document, to support the new owner's claim to ownership. All real estate is a non-probate asset, except for entireties property and life estates, which are not includable in the estate, and real estate left to the estate to be sold, which is a probate asset.

## Why It Matters how the Property is Classified

Classification matters because of the way assets are used to pay estate debts. Probate assets are used first to pay the bills. If there are enough probate assets to pay all claims, costs of administration, court costs, attorney costs, and Personal Representative's commission, then Will bequests can be paid and the rest (the "residuary") can be distributed to the heirs. But, if there is not enough money from the probate assets, then the Personal Representative must reach out and pull one or more of the non-probate assets back into the estate to generate cash to pay the bills.

**Example.** When John Auten died, he had $200,000 in

probate assets, and three heirs, his children. He also had $1,000,000 in non-probate assets--$500,000 in his brokerage account (all three children were joint beneficiaries), $275,000 in the value in his home and $225,000 in life insurance (only George was the beneficiary). Counting funeral expenses, estate costs and unsecured bank loans, total claims against his estate were $350,000.00. George must now decide what non-probate asset to bring back into the estate to generate the additional $150,000 needed to pay all of the bills.

## Personal Responsibility for the Personal Representative

The Personal Representative is personally responsible to make sure the estate assets are gathered, the bills and costs paid, and the remainder is properly distributed. Since creditors have 90 days to file their claims, a prudent Personal Representative should hold all assets of the estate until the claims period closes.

**Example.** Fred Golightly died leaving three heirs (his three children), probate assets worth $750,000 (primarily from his successful brokerage account), no real estate or other non-probate assets. His son, Jim is Personal Representative. After the Notice to Creditors has been running for 60 days, with no unexpected claims filed or even hinted at, Jim's brother, Cain, has a business emergency and convinces Jim to advance him $100,000 of his share of the estate. Jim gives him the money. On day 89 of the claim period, the Securities and Exchange Commission files notice of a claim against Fred for insider trading, and, ultimately, Fred's estate ends up owing a $600,000 fine, not to mention the $150,000 spent on attorney's fees defending this action. The estate only has $500,000 left to pay the fine with ($750,000 minus $150,000 to attorneys minus $100,000 to Cain). Jim is personally liable for the $100,000 he distributed to an heir before making sure all claims and costs had been paid.

## Summary to This Point in the Probate

While you catch your breath, here's a summary of what it took to get the Probate estate through the first 90 days:

Several days or weeks after the decedent dies, the family gathers the death certificate, Will, if there is one, information about all assets the decedent had an interest in, and visits with the probate attorney.

The probate attorney reviews all of the documents, helps the family decide whether a probate is needed, outlines the scope of work involved, and, hopefully, quotes a reasonable fixed fee to assist with the probate work.

The person who will be the Personal Representative is selected, court documents drafted, including the Initial Inventory, filed and published, as needed, by the attorney. A hearing is held, the Personal Representative is appointed by the clerk of court, the Personal Representative signs his Oath, and posts

Bond, if required. The Clerk issues Letters Testamentary to the Personal Representative.

The Personal Representative, or attorney, publishes the Notice to Creditors. The Personal Representative, using his Letters, gathers all assets he knows about or can discover, and waits for unknown claims to be filed within the 90 day claim period. The Personal Representative may wish to consult with the estate attorney about dubious claims that the Personal Representative wants to deny and the possible problems with doing that.

OK, and now, as Paul Harvey used to say "For the rest of the story."

The Personal Representative must work diligently to find all of the decedent's assets, because he must file a more complete inventory within 90 days after filing the Initial Inventory.

## The 90 Day Inventory

This inventory, not surprisingly, is called the 90 Day Inventory. The Personal Representative has had a full three months to locate any and all assets of the decedent, including bank accounts, brokerage accounts, vehicle titles, pay checks, dividend checks, retirement checks, money stuffed under the mattress, and anything paid to the decedent by his debtors or that is still owed but unpaid. Hopefully, the Personal

Representative has found all of the decedent's assets by now.

In the ideal estate, once the 90 day claims period has expired and the 90 day inventory has been done, it would seem a simple thing to pay all the claims and bequests, calculate the heirs' share of the remainder and distribute that to them; get receipts from the heirs, close the estate checking account, receive the final checking account statement with the last of the cashed checks; prepare the Final Accounting; file the court papers to have a final hearing before the Clerk of Court; have the hearing and receive the Personal Representative's release from office.

But, many things can cause a delay in the completion in the probate. Typical reasons for delay include:

- The family or the attorney have difficulties in determining all of the assets and liabilities of the probate
- Someone contests the probate or disagrees how the probate is being handled (this could cause completion of a probate to be delayed for years)
- Either the attorney, an heir or the Personal Representative procrastinate
- A federal estate tax return must be filed. This requires that certain probate assets be appraised and often requires that assets be sold to pay the tax. The federal estate tax return is due nine months after the death of the decedent and

often the probate is not concluded until federal estate tax matters are concluded.

If the estate is going to be open beyond one year from the date of the decedent's death, an Annual Accounting must be filed. This accounting, simply put, shows the court, in detail, what assets have come in, what bills have been paid and what assets are still on hand. Frequently, this is not as simple as it sounds because values put on items on the Initial Inventory may have gone up or down when they were ultimately disposed of, and this change in value must also be accounted for. When combined with the newly discovered assets shown on the 90 day inventory, the arithmetic can become complex and confusing in a hurry.

If the estate can be closed within the first year, the Final Accounting covers the same items as an Annual Accounting, but including final distributions also.

## Does a Probate Take a Long Time?

It is reported in many national publications that probate takes many years to conclude. Many of these publications are also advocating the use of some probate avoidance tool.

In North Carolina, our probate laws are simpler than the laws of many other states. Probates with absolutely no complications can take about seven months to complete. An average timeline follows:

- January 1 – date of death
- January 15 – meet with attorney
- January 25 – supply all information requested to attorney
- February 15 – family meets with attorney to sign necessary documents
- February 20 – documents filed at courthouse
- February 28 – clerk of court appoints Personal Representative (add two more weeks for intestate estates)
- March 5 -- Notice to Creditors first published
- May 28 -- the 90 Day Inventory is Due
- June 5 -- Creditor claim filing period expires
- June 15-- Personal Representative finishes paying all claims, bequests and distribution to heirs, closes checking account
- July 1 – Personal Representative received final checking account statement and cancelled checks
- July 10 – Personal Representative finishes Final Accounting, file for final hearing before Clerk of court
- July 30 -- Final hearing held, Account approved, Personal Representative released from office.

## Probate Costs

Probate costs can vary from probate to probate, and from attorney to attorney. Attorney fees and court filing fees are a part of every probate. Some probates incur accounting fees, appraisal fees, Federal estate tax, and other costs.

Some probates only include a house, a vehicle and perhaps a bank account or two. If all heirs are in agreement and the information on the deceased's assets is organized, it should be less expensive than other probates.

Other probates are much more expensive. When heirs choose to fight their differences out in court, the costs can be staggering.

Court filing fees are the same for each County in North Carolina. Attorney fees will vary from attorney to attorney. Unlike some other states, North Carolina has no statutory attorney fee schedule. North Carolina attorneys are required to charge a "reasonable fee." Common examples of fee structures include:

- Hourly rate billing. The attorney will charge an hourly rate. This doesn't help you out because the consumer has no idea how many hours the probate will billed for at the end
- Fixed fee. This is where the attorney designates either a fixed amount or a fixed percentage of the estate to perform the services to be rendered. Consumers like this because they know in advance the fee and the attorney is rewarded for his or her efficiency.

Whatever you do, make sure you have an agreement in writing with the attorney so that you will not be unpleasantly surprised later with an invoice that knocks your socks off.

## Minimizing Problems and Delays with a Probate

Potential Creditors' Claims

In North Carolina, if no Notice of Creditors is ever published, unsecured creditors have up to three years to file a claim against the decedent (even if the creditor has to open the estate himself). With the Personal Representative's ability to pull non-probate assets back into the estate to pay claims, this leaves almost every asset exposed for the entire three year period.

In order to minimize the cost and inconvenience of probate, one approach is:

First, own only non-probate assets such as IRAs, 401(k)s and annuities. Or,

Second, form a revocable living trust and transfer all of your probate assets to your trust before you die. Your trust will own your home, other real estate, bank and investment accounts, and any other asset previously titled in your name. When you die, your assets are titled in the name of your trust.

Third, your estate is probated, but all of your assets have already been transferred to the people you designated. There is no delay on access or ownership, because the Trustee was the owner. There is very little for the probate court to control or charge for. The paperwork is reduced, and, by publishing the Notice to Creditors, claims can be cut off relatively quickly. No beneficiary will be inconvenienced because the probate has not been finished.

Is this as good as being in a State where probate can be entirely avoided by the use of revocable trusts? No, not really. But it is the safest route in North Carolina to ensure nothing unexpected pops up six or twelve or even thirty months down the road.

## Out of State Real Estate

The probate of a North Carolina resident governs all of the financial accounts and other "movable" property, wherever located, but it governs the real estate located only in North Carolina and not the real estate located in any other state.

If a North Carolina resident owns real estate in another state, something called an ancillary probate will be required in that other state where they owned property. Each state's ancillary probate laws are different, but an ancillary probate procedure typically includes filing a certified copy of the last will and testament in that state, along with other paperwork required. Often the family is required to hire an attorney in that other state to oversee that ancillary probate. For an out of state decedent, ancillary probate in North Carolina requires the same steps, paperwork and time as a probate for a North Carolina decedent.

Owning significant real estate in other states can be a reason to transfer that property to an entity such as a limited liability company or a revocable living trust, so that multiple ancillary probates can be avoided in states that have a burdensome probate process.

## Contesting the Probate

Most probates are uncontested. The family member dies, the probate is handled, the property is transferred to the heirs, and families move on.

Some probates, however, are contested. It's unfortunate when heirs disagree. Often, no one wins. There's a common saying: "If you want to get to really know someone, share an inheritance with them."

There are a number of reasons why probates are contested. Some of them include:

• A person contests the validity or interpretation of the last will and testament

- An heir feels that the Personal Representative is either not listing all of the probate assets and debts properly, or the heir feels that the Personal Representative is not acting appropriately
- The heirs just don't like or trust each other (not a valid reason)

## Compensation of Personal Representative

If there is no provision in the Will to the contrary, or no other agreement between the parties, the Personal Representative is allowed a fee of five percent of the probate assets coming into the estate. In many probates, a family member is the executor or administrator, and that family member may waive this fee either because they are willing to do it for free because they are an heir and it's a family matter, or since the probate representative's fee is subject to income tax, he feels satisfied receiving his inheritance which typically is not subject to income tax.

## Conclusion

A North Carolina probate is required when a person dies and the individual had certain property titled in his or name on the date of death. The probate is the process of transferring assets from the deceased's name to the heirs. Although North Carolina may have a simple and easy probate process when compared to other states, the process itself is neither simple nor easy. There are many decisions to be made, few of which can be knowingly made by a layman without experience in this area. Unless you are experienced with probate work, a consultation with an estate administration attorney might be money well spent.

# CHAPTER 11

# NONPROBATE ASSETS
### These are important and often overlooked

It is likely that you own nonprobate assets. Nonprobate assets are assets that do not pass pursuant to your Will when you die. Common nonprobate assets include your retirement accounts (such as your IRA or 401(k)), life insurance, and annuities. It is important that you monitor these assets during your lifetime and properly designate your beneficiaries.

Maybe you are like some people that have the bulk of their life savings in nonprobate assets. Perhaps you worked for a company that had a 401(k) plan. When you retired, you rolled your 401(k) plan assets into an individual retirement account (IRA). You take monthly or annual distributions from your IRA to pay for your retirement. Your other assets include your home and some smaller accounts outside of your IRA.

Perhaps you are married and your spouse has children from a

prior marriage. You set up a Will and designate that all your assets go to your children when you die. However, you fail to realize that your spouse is named the primary beneficiary of your IRA – your biggest asset by far. When you die, your children don't get any of your IRA even though you wrote a Will designating that your children receive all of your assets when you die. What's worse is that after your death, your spouse rolls your IRA over into his or her IRA and when your spouse later dies, that spouse's IRA goes to his or her children (or perhaps his or her new spouse).

For many people, properly designating beneficiaries on nonprobate assets is just as important, if not more important, than creating a Will or revocable living trust. Failing to properly designate your beneficiaries on nonprobate assets could result in your life savings being transferred to people other than those closest to you.

The following are examples of common nonprobate assets along with what you can do to make sure that your wishes are carried out.

### Retirement accounts

Retirement accounts include Keogh pensions, profit-sharing or stock bonus plans qualified under the Internal Revenue Code, an individual retirement account (IRA), a Roth IRA, or a tax-sheltered annuity.

Traditional families often don't encounter problems with IRAs. Traditional families are those where the two parents had children together, and all members of the family agree that when one spouse dies, the surviving spouse should own the IRA, and when the surviving spouse dies, the IRA will be divided equally among the children. The spouse is typically named the primary beneficiary and all of their children are named the contingent beneficiaries.

The problem occurs when the family circumstances vary from the traditional. Often, individuals go into great detail when having their Wills prepared so that spouses, children, and other loved ones are protected. But little, if any, attention is given to the beneficiary designation forms on the retirement accounts.

**Example.** Jack had two children from his prior marriage. Jack is currently married to Rachel. Jack sets up his Will so that Rachel gets the lifetime income from Jack's entire estate, and Jack names his two children as the owners of the remainder. Jack has an IRA valued at $600,000, while his other assets (his interest in the home and other financial accounts) total $300,000. When Jack died, Rachel received Jack's entire $600,000 IRA because she was the primary beneficiary while Jack's children were merely the contingent beneficiaries. Rachel received the lifetime use of the $300,000 of assets that passed pursuant to Jack's Will. Rachel is free to do whatever she wants with his IRA, including leave it to her children (not Jack's children) or leave it to the husband she marries after Jack dies.

If Jack wanted his children to benefit from his IRA, he could have named them as a primary beneficiary of part or all of the IRA (for example, 25% to each of his two children and 50% to his wife, Rachel), or he could have named a trust as the primary beneficiary of his IRA. The trust instrument would likely have allowed Rachel to use the IRA during her lifetime and then at her death, the remainder of the IRA in trust would go back to Jack's children (not Rachel's beneficiaries).

If you name a trust as the beneficiary of your IRA, be aware that there are numerous hurdles involving income tax, minimum required distributions, and trust accounting, but doing it properly can allow you to provide for all of your loved ones regardless of your family circumstances.

### Life insurance

Life insurance proceeds, generally, are income tax free to the beneficiaries. Life insurance is also a nonprobate asset. When you purchase a life insurance policy, you are asked to name a beneficiary on the life insurance company's beneficiary designation form. Even if your Will states that you want your life insurance to go to your children or your spouse, the life insurance company will only pay the proceeds to the beneficiary who is designated on the beneficiary designation form, regardless of what your Will provides.

Similar to the way your retirement accounts should be handled, if you want your spouse to benefit from your life insurance, and you want to designate who gets the remaining funds when your spouse dies, you should consider naming a trust as the beneficiary. Otherwise, your spouse will be free to leave that money to whomever he or she wishes (which may or may not be the same people you would want to have it).

## Annuities

Annuities also are distributed after your death to the named beneficiaries. If you own annuities, make certain that you've properly documented your beneficiaries. Many annuity owners die without fully understanding how the nonprobate assets are to be distributed. Some of these people may be rolling over in their graves right now.

## Conclusion

Failing to properly designate beneficiaries on nonprobate assets is one of the costliest and most-overlooked aspects of estate planning.

If you have nonprobate assets such as retirement accounts, life insurance, and annuities, consider the following:

- Review your primary and contingent beneficiaries regularly
- If you are married and you have children from a prior marriage, consider designating a trust as the beneficiary of nonprobate assets. This will allow you, for example, to provide for your surviving spouse and also provide who benefits from the trust assets after the death of your surviving spouse.
- You can designate multiple primary beneficiaries. For example, your spouse may be a 50% beneficiary, and your children may each be 25% beneficiaries
- If you name a trust or someone other than your spouse as the primary beneficiary of your retirement accounts, be aware of the income tax consequences as well as the often-changing rules regarding minimum required distributions

# CHAPTER 12

# ESTATE PLANNING LETTER OF LAST INSTRUCTIONS
## Make it easy for your loved ones

While it is important that the proper estate planning legal documents be in place, it is also important that other informal items be properly documented.

Examples of additional items that should be documented include:

- Your wishes regarding your personal effects
- Who to notify upon your death
- Your desired funeral arrangements
- The location of your personal papers
- Access to your vehicle titles and registration
- Recent statements of bank and investment accounts
- Location and key to safe deposit boxes
- List of your debts
- Property descriptions for real estate you own

- List of survivor's benefits
- List of websites, User IDs and Passwords

## Personal effects

The disposition of your personal effects, such as furniture, jewelry, art, guns, tools, clothing, photographs, and other nontitled assets can be one of the most difficult things for your heirs to handle. While it's easy for your two children to divide up the money that's in your bank account, it's not so simple for children to divide your family portraits or other family heirlooms.

Disposing of your personal effects can be done generally in one of two ways. First, you could specify who you want to get your personal items in your last will and testament. This is often not recommended because you have to include a detailed list of your personal effects in your Will, and then if you want to add, delete, or change one of these bequests, you have to go through the formal process of changing your Will.

An alternative to listing your personal effects in your Will is to create a less formal set of instructions to your heirs where you personally and in writing, let them know how you want your personal effects distributed. It may be in your own handwriting or it might be something you type on the computer. The idea is not to make a formal document, but an informal request to your heirs about how to divide these items that often do not have significant market value, but have tremendous sentimental value.

**Example.** Maria has a daughter and two sons. In her Will, she provided that all of her assets were to go equally to her three children. After she had her Will prepared by an attorney, she sat down and prepared a letter to her children stating which personal effects she wanted to go to each child and grandchild. While this informal letter was not a valid legal document, Maria's children honored her requests after she died and divided all of the personal effects in accordance with her wishes.

While this informal method of distributing personal effects is simple and works particularly well when all of the heirs are close, be aware, however, that if you want to make absolutely certain that your wishes are followed, you need to consider expressly stating your wishes in your Will.

## List of assets

You should take certain actions now so that your loved ones will have an easier time settling your affairs when you are gone. One of the things you can do is complete a detailed list of your assets and liabilities. Keep this list with your other important estate planning documents and update it annually. When you die, your family will have to produce this information to the probate attorney, and it will be much easier for them to access the necessary information if you've left them a complete list of your assets and debts. Your list of assets should include:

- Real estate. A legal description of each piece of real estate that you own. Since your North Carolina Deeds are on record in the county courthouse, just a list of properties, the owner's name (it might be your LLC or Trust), their street addresses and what County they are in. For out of State properties, list owner's name, legal description, address, County or other information needed to locate the ownership records in that other state.

- Bank accounts. An itemized listing of bank accounts that you have an ownership interest in.

- Investments. A listing of investment accounts and copies of stock certificates that you own.

- Vehicles. Copies of car titles that you own.

- Debts. A list of your creditors, such as mortgage companies, banks, and credit card companies.

- Other important information. Also include with this list of assets information regarding your funeral arrangements, the location and contents of your safe deposit boxes, and the location and status of any life insurance policies on which you are the owner or the insured.

- The newest addition to this list is a list of Web sites like Face Book, Drop Box, financial institutions and other internet locations where you might have information, pictures or important data stored, and include your current User ID and Password for each site. If you don't, your family might lose a whole generation worth of photos, genealogy data or actual cash money because no one else has access to your accounts.

## Conclusion

Properly documenting your assets during your lifetime, and informally providing for the disposition of your personal effects may be just as important as having the proper estate planning legal documents in place.

Make a list of your assets and debts and keep it updated annually. Let your executor that you named in your Will know how to access this information.

If you want to avoid a squabble among your heirs over your personal effects such as family pictures, furniture, jewelry, and other personal items, write an informal letter to them instructing them on how to divide those items. When they see that you've documented what you wanted, they will be inclined to honor your wishes.

# CHAPTER 13

# GET STARTED
### It's not as painful as you might think

Because of the uncertainties of life, it's never too early to begin estate planning. Having a proper estate plan can be one of the best things you can do for the loved ones you leave behind.

Estate planning is not painful. You will not get pricked or prodded. Once your estate planning is up to date, you'll have peace of mind knowing that you've done what is necessary to have your affairs in order.

To get started, take the following steps:

### Find an Attorney

There are a number of different ways you can find a competent attorney. Some of these include:

- Ask your friends, neighbors and relatives who they know

that could help them with their estate plan. If they had a good experience using a certain attorney, it's likely that you'll also have a good experience.

- Many attorneys are listed in the telephone book or on the internet. While a referral from a trusted source is the best bet, you will be able to find a number of attorneys in the yellow pages or on the internet. Make sure that they list estate planning as a significant part of their practice.

## Meet with the Attorney

Many attorneys will offer to meet with you in an initial meeting without you incurring any cost. This is a great way for you to get to know the attorney and to find out whether you'd want to work with him or her. You'll be able to ask questions, and the attorney will likely make certain recommendations to you in order to complete your estate plan. The attorney should also be able to give you a quote or an estimate regarding the fees you will be required to pay. Don't ever retain an attorney without first having a thorough understanding of how you will be charged.

## Be Prepared

Once you've located your attorney, it is helpful if you provide him with a general list of your assets and their values. The attorney will be able to determine if there is any special planning that will be necessary to reduce potential tax.

When you meet with the attorney, be prepared to answer the following questions:

If you're married, how do you want to leave assets to your spouse? Do you want to leave your spouse full ownership or do you want to leave your spouse just a life estate? Or perhaps you want to leave assets in trust for your spouse.

How do you want to leave assets to your children? Do you want to leave assets to them outright or in trust? If you leave assets to your children in trust, who will be the trustee and under what circumstances can your children use the trust principal?

Do you want to leave a bequest to your grandchildren? Some grandparents want to leave a bequest to their grandchildren, while others want to leave it all to their children. There is no right or wrong way to do it.

Do you want to leave a bequest to charity?

Who will serve as your executor? If you're married, you may want your spouse to be your executor, and you may want an adult child to be your alternate executor.

Who do you want to handle your financial affairs for you during your lifetime in the event that you can't do it for yourself?

Who do you want making your medical decisions for you if you are unable?

Do you want to sign a living will whereby you declare your intentions regarding life support machines?

Once you answer these and other questions, your attorney should have the necessary information to draft the appropriate estate planning documents. These documents typically include your last will and testament, your power of attorney, your health care power of attorney, your living will, and perhaps trusts or other documents.

Once you're satisfied with the documents, you will sign them, typically in the presence of your attorney (who is a notary) and two witnesses.

In addition to signing the necessary estate planning documents that are customized by your attorney, you also need to make certain that all necessary beneficiary designation forms are properly completed on your non-probate assets.

## Storing Your Estate Planning Documents

Keep your signed, original last will and testament in a safe place. Some people keep their Will in a bank safe deposit box, while other people keep their Will in their home. The attorney should keep a photocopy of your Will.

Let your executor know where your original Will is located. If you keep it in a safe deposit box, make sure that you complete the necessary paperwork at the bank so that your trusted friend or relative can access the box after your death without having to get the courts involved.

### Review Your Estate Plan

Don't make the common mistake of completing your estate plan, and then having it collect dust for many years. Your circumstances are likely to change over the years and your estate plan needs to keep up with your changing circumstances. Meet with your attorney about every three to five years or more often if any of the following occur:

- One of your heirs has died
- There is a significant change in the value of what you own
- You change your mind about how you will leave your assets to your heirs
- You want to change your executor or you want to change your power of attorney
- You discover there is a change in the law that may affect you
- You get married or divorced
- You incur a life-threatening illness
- You move into or out of the state

## Conclusion

In estate planning, North Carolina's laws are far different from the laws of many other states. To complete and maintain a proper estate plan, do the following:

- Find an attorney that you are comfortable with – particularly one that specializes in the complex field of estate planning
- Be prepared to provide the attorney with information about what you own.
- Be prepared to answer the attorney's questions about how you want to leave your assets behind, as well as questions regarding who you would want making important financial and medical decisions for you when you are unable to make them for yourself
- Make certain you execute the proper estate planning legal documents as well as beneficiary designation forms
- Store your documents so that your trusted friends, relatives, and advisors have access to them upon your disability or your death
- Review your estate plan periodically so that it can be updated as your circumstances change

Congratulations! You should now be informed enough so that you can undertake this important task of estate planning. Once you have an up to date estate plan, you'll have peace of mind knowing you've done what's necessary to protect yourself and your loved ones, and you can continue to enjoy your life!

# GLOSSARY

**Administrator** – the person appointed by the court whose duty it is to collect, preserve and manage the property of a decedent's estate. The court often appoints an administrator when a decedent had no last will and testament

**Advancement** – the addition of the value of gifted property, received by one heir, to the value of all property in the estate in order that estate property can be divided equally among all of the heirs. People often provide in their Wills that lifetime gifts are not to be treated as advancements.

**Beneficiary** – a person named in your Last Will who will inherit property from you

**Entireties Property** – real estate held in the name of both husband and wife. North Carolina statutes presume they intend for the survivor to inherit all of the property, unless the parties specify otherwise.

**Estate Administration** – the process of settling an estate after someone dies

**Executor** – the person you designate in your last will and testament who will work with the attorney to settle your estate

**Estate Planning** – the process of arranging your affairs so that upon your death or disability, your estate will be managed efficiently by the people you trust, and there will be minimal costs of probate, tax, long term care, or other costs

**Estate Tax** – the tax your estate must pay to the federal government if your net estate exceeds the applicable estate tax exemption at your death

**Gift Tax** – tax you must pay to the state or federal government for making a gift for the benefit of another person

**Guardian** – the person who is appointed by the court to be the legal caretaker of: children under the age of eighteen; the financial affairs of an adult the court has declared incompetent to manager his/her own financial affairs; the personal affairs of an adult the court has declared incompetent to take care of themselves

**Heir** – a person who inherits from you when you do not have a last will and testament. The people you name in your Will to inherit from you, in North Carolina, are called beneficiaries

**Holographic Will** –It is entirely in your own handwriting, signed and dated. Holographic wills are not recommended because lay people typically do not have the expertise to prepare such an important legal document as your last will and testament

**Inheritance Tax** – the amount of tax owed to the State of North Carolina by your heirs when they inherit from you. This tax no longer exists.

**Intestate Laws** – the laws that dictate who inherits your assets if you die without a valid last will and testament.

**Last Will and Testament** – a legal document naming your executor and describing, among other things, who is entitled to your assets when you die.

**Life Estate** – the right to use an asset for as long as the life estate holder lives

**Living Trust** – a trust that you establish during your lifetime

**Living Will** – a document whereby you express your intentions regarding the withdrawal or withholding of life support systems

**Medicaid** – the federal and state program that will pay for all or a portion of your nursing home care if you meet the Medicaid eligibility requirements

**Medicaid Planning** – the process of taking advantage of legal strategies to protect your estate in the event you need long term care in a nursing home

**Medicare** – completely different from Medicaid. Medicare is health insurance for most senior citizens, paying most of the cost for surgeries, doctor visits, and other medical expenses

**Nonprobate assets** – assets that are not listed in a probate, such as qualified retirement plans, individual retirement accounts, life insurance, and annuities

**Personal Representative** – the term applied to the person in charge of the decedent's estate. Also known as Executor, Executrix (in a Will) or Administrator, Administratrix (no Will).

**Power of Attorney** – a document you sign authorizing another to act for you during your lifetime

**Probate** – the court-supervised process of transferring your assets to your heirs or legatees after your death.

**Remainderman** – the person who holds the remaining interest in an asset after the life estate holder dies

**Revocable Living Trust** – a type of trust you create during your lifetime, whereby you are the trustee and beneficiary during your lifetime, and you provide who the beneficiaries are at your death. Often used as a Will substitute to avoid probate.

**Self-Proving Will** - Self-proving wills are typically typed, they have certain required language, and they are formally notarized and witnessed. Because they are witnessed and notarized, no additional testimony from the witnesses is required to admit this will to probate.

**Separate Property** – property that you own that is not entireties property with your spouse. Common examples of separate property are property you hold title to in just your name, such as bank accounts, real estate or brokerage accounts.

**Settlor** – a person who creates a trust.

**Probate** – the court-supervised process of transferring your assets to your heirs after you die.

**Testamentary Trust** – a trust, the terms of which are stated in your last will and testament. Parents with minor children often establish testamentary trusts in their Wills.

**Trust** – a relationship resulting from the transfer of title to property to a person (trustee) to be administered for the benefit of another (beneficiary)

**Trustee** – the person who manages the assets of the trust for the beneficiaries.

**Will** – also known as last your will and testament. Your Will is the important document that you sign which leaves your estate to your loved ones, names your executor, and provides for many other aspects regarding the settling of your estate. It must be signed by the testator and witnessed by two independent witnesses. To be admitted to probate, these witnesses must appear in court or sign notarized statements saying they saw the testator sign the Will, among other things. If they cannot be found, admitting the Will becomes more difficult.

# THE LAST WORD

Early in my estate planning career, I prepared the documents for a middle aged couple who has three small children. Once they were ready, I called the house, on a Thursday, to schedule a time for them to come in and sign everything. The wife answered and I suggested the next day for them to come in. She said "Oh, my husband has a little cold, but will be better by Monday. Can we do it then?" I said yes, we set the time, and hung up. On Monday, they didn't show for their appointment, so I called the house again. Only to discover that the husband had unexpectedly died over the weekend. No Will, owning a house, with minor children. The stay at home mom ultimately had to pay a lawyer to get Court approval to sell the house, which she could no longer afford, in order to move closer to her parents. The children's share of the sale proceeds had to be accounted for each year until each turned 18. And then the child was entitled to receive his share in full.

Recently, I was working with an elderly couple, second marriage for both. Both had substantial assets and children from their first marriage. The husband's children were "worthless" (his term) and we were working on a Revocable Trust for each of them that would allow the survivor of the husband and wife full access to the decedent's assets, while protecting them from any claims from the husband's children.

While husband and wife were trying to come up with the perfect solution, the wife died. Even with her health issues, death is always unexpected.

Whether it's a long slow decline, like Terri Shiavo or Casey Kasem, or the quickest, most painless exit possible, it will happen to all of us. You can't prevent it, but you can plan for it, and protect yourself and your loved ones. **Get started now.**

Contact me at:
Eric@KindbergEstateLaw.com or 704-507-6444.

Already have an estate planning attorney? Then call them. But do it today.

# NOTES